The Second Christianity

D0844046

April 22, 1986

JOHN HICK

The Second
Christianity

SCM PRESS LTD

334 01484 0

Earlier editions published as
Christianity at the Centre 1968
and *The Centre of Christianity* 1977
This edition first published 1983
by SCM Press Ltd
26–30 Tottenham Road, London N1

Typeset by Gloucester Typesetting Services
and printed in Great Britain by
Richard Clay Ltd (The Chaucer Press)
Bungay, Suffolk

Contents

Preface

The first edition of this book, under the title *Christianity at the Centre*, appeared in 1968, just as I was moving from a teaching post in the Faculty of Divinity at Cambridge to one in the Department of Theology at Birmingham University. The second edition, in 1977, under the title *The Centre of Christianity*, came after I had been immersed for some years in the multi-cultural, multi-faith city of Birmingham. This third version, with yet another title, coincides with another move, into the ferment of religious studies and the interaction of Eastern and Western traditions in southern California.

These fifteen years since 1968 have brought discernible changes on the Christian scene. The last fifteen years are, of course, part of the larger span since the Second World War. But the trends of that longer period have become particularly evident within this last decade and a half. In very broad terms, the total human situation, as we have been conscious of it in the West, has become increasingly complex, baffling, and threatening. We are less and less confident that it is under human control. The world seems to be in an intensifying state of multiple danger. And this sense of uncertainty and peril has evoked two opposite reactions, constituting a majority and a minority outlook.

The majority outlook is a concentration of attention and allegiance on one's own familiar 'tribe', finding comfort and strength in the fellowship of one's in-group over against the out-groups. Politically, this has expressed itself in firm policies of national self-interest and in a resurgence of us-against-them patriotism – recently dramatically displayed, within both Britain and Argentina, in the brief but bloody war in the South Atlantic. Religiously, a parallel response to the bewildering complexity of our contemporary perception of the human situation has expressed itself in the revival of a simplified pre-modern Christianity. The Bible is seen as uniquely inspired and authoritive, and the Christian world-view is accordingly identified with that of the late first-century church. Within this world-view the gospel is an offer of personal salvation and a call to us-against-them religious patriotism. In the United States the alliance between conservative religion and right wing politics is open and blatant; in Britain it is no less real, but more discreet and pervasive.

The other, minority, response looks in the opposite direction, gripped by the vision of our one world and our common humanity. It is accordingly deeply concerned about the global problems of the threat of nuclear destruction, the squandering of our precious energy resources, the North-South, white-black divide, Third World poverty and deprivation, the world population explosion. And it tends to see the great religious traditions of the world – Christianity, Buddhism, Islam, Hinduism, Taoism, African primal religion – as representing different awarenesses of and different responses to a divine Reality which transcends all our human thoughts and images, scriptures and cults.

The polarity of these two opposite responses breaks down, of course, in practice in that many people move between them, adopting one outlook at one time or in one context, and the other at other times or in other contexts. For we are all to some degree divided and confused. But still the polarity is there, and it produces the 'two Christianities' referred to in Chapter III.

This book attempts to describe the religious core of 'the second Christianity' – the Christianity which is not the tribal religion of one section of humanity over against the rest, but rather one way amongst others of living out our common humanity in relation to a divine Presence which grasps us all.

Department of Religion,   JOHN HICK
Claremont Graduate School,
Claremont, California 91711

Introduction: Humanism or Christianity?

It has become obvious that we are living at a turning point in the history of Christianity. This is mainly because the development of modern science has made incredible much of the content of traditional Christian belief.

Here I have in mind such beliefs as that man was originally created finitely perfect but fell through his own wrong choice into sin and misery; that God intervenes from time to time in history by miraculously suspending the laws of nature; that Christ was born of a virgin mother, lived on earth as a divine being with omnipotent power and omniscient mind, made atonement by his death for human sin, and that after his death his corpse came back to life; that the Bible is the infallible, divinely inspired record of all this; that eternal heaven or hell awaits us after death.

The question today is whether such beliefs are of the permanent essence of Christianity; or whether they belong to the history of its interaction with the prescientific culture which has only recently come to an end. If the former, Christianity is doomed to the role of a fading superstition. But if the latter, these mythical concepts can properly be left behind as Christianity advances into the new cultural world of modern science.

In this situation one option for the Christian is to stand by the traditional system of beliefs, regarding it as of the essence of the faith. This is the response of the growing and articulate conservative wing of the churches which today calls itself evangelical. This conservative response has become a major phenomenon. Indeed it is probable that today the main cleavage within Christianity is no longer between the denominations – for their differences are at least in process of being bridged – but between 'evangelicals' and 'radicals' regardless of denomination. Radical Anglicans, Roman Catholics, and, say, Presbyterians have in many ways more in common with one another than with the conservatives within their respective churches; while conservative Presbyterians, Roman Catholics and Anglicans have more in common with one another than with their respective radical brethren. One can only view with dismay the prospect of an increasing polarization along this axis, leading each party to exaggerated self-consciousness over against the other.

I am not going to argue in detail against the conservative option here. Although very many intelligent and responsible Christians for whom I have the greatest respect see the classic structure and proportions of theology that we have inherited from the time of St Augustine as being permanently valid and as of the essence of the Christian faith, I am quite unable to share their view. However, I do not want to expend my main effort as a theologian in criticizing traditional theology. For the 'liberal' attack upon orthodoxy is as irrelevant to the real issues of the future as is that which it attacks. (It has, however, to be acknowledged that within the life of the churches individuals who cannot accept the officially approved formulae will still sometimes be forced by militant conservatism to take a stand on some of these ultimately irrelevant issues. Indeed I was myself involved in such a case in 1961 and 1962 when some of the fundamentalist brethren sought to exclude me from the ministry of the United Presbyterian Church, USA, because I do not affirm the doctrine of the Virgin Birth.) It is more important today to seek for a viable Christian theology for the late twentieth century which will avoid anachronisms while preserving the living reality of Christian faith. This book is one of many today in which an attempt is being made to do this.

But first we must face the challenge of contemporary Humanism, with its claim that our life can be satisfactorily lived and understood on the assumption that there is no God.

I do not believe that the existence of God can be proved – although I do believe (as is developed in chapter II, section 3) that a belief in God's reality, based on religious experience, can be an entirely rational conviction; and also (as is developed in chapter V below) that the reality of God will eventually, in the final completion of the creative process, be evident to all. But at this point I should like to focus attention upon something which most Christians and most Humanists agree in regarding as a supremely important value – namely, self-giving love. What is the status of this ideal?

For traditional Christianity, it reflects the nature of the sovereign power of being. It is supported and its ultimate fulfilment guaranteed by the structure of reality. But for the Humanist it is only a thought in the mind, or an agitation in the brain, of members of the organic species homo sapiens. It did not exist before this particular form of animal life had emerged within the evolutionary process nor will it exist after human life has eventually perished. The existence of God, with which in Christian belief it is bound up, is only the existence of a modification of consciousness in a fleeting form of organic life on the surface of one of the planets of a small star in one of the many millions of galaxies. If, as is entirely possible, there is intelligent life on other planets elsewhere in the universe, and if such life has also formed the idea of deity, then this idea has occurred more widely than we are at present aware; but its status remains the same – it is simply an idea in a number of streams of consciousness which are precariously dependent upon fleeting animal organisms. It is still not, according to Humanism, a true idea in the sense of corresponding to a reality external to the consciousnesses which entertain it. For the idea of God is the idea of an eternal at-least-personal Being who has created everything that exists other than himself; but there is, according to Humanism, no such Being. And the ideal of self-giving love has a similarly unsupported status. It may never have been exemplified in human life, and it may likewise never come to be exemplified. It has no cosmic status or backing. Like the idea of God, it is simply a thought or a sentiment in the consciousness excreted by a brief combination of nerve cells.

This humanistic view entails a profoundly tragic conception of human life, a conception which becomes most acutely evident at two points. First, there is the boundary situation of death. On this view death is final; and the character of conscious life must be affected by the knowledge of its finality. For Humanists believe that our highest ideals and hopes are destined never to be fulfilled either in our own lives or in the corporate life of the race. It is this inevitable final fruitlessness of man's ideals and hopes that renders our human situation so tragic. We achieve some measure of love or wisdom or knowledge or creativity or community, and desire to progress indefinitely in the deeper fulfilment of these possibilities. For there seems in principle to be no limit to the development of the valuable aspects of human nature and human existence in the realms of personal relationship, scientific understanding, artistic enjoyment and contemplative vision. But if the humanistic philosophy is true these aspirations are delusory; for they can never be fulfilled. They would be appropriate to beings made for eternal life in a universe designed for the development of personal values; but to fleeting animal organisms they can add only the tragic and pathetic dignity of a grand delusion.

The tragedy is almost immeasurably intensified by the problem of human suffering. It is difficult for us who inhabit the affluent regions of North America, Western Europe or Australasia to realize that most of the human race today is living in desperate poverty, undernourishment and disease. And if we try to think of the millions of millions of human lives that have been lived since the beginning of human existence, the amount of pain, anguish, fear, sorrow, dread, jealousy, rage, bereavement and anxiety that has been suffered numbs the imagination. According to Humanism, this vast extent of past human suffering is simply an ultimate fact. Nothing is being or can ever be done about it. There is no possibility of good being brought out of this evil; for the sufferers have long since ceased to exist. We ourselves may be fortunate enough to be among the few who enjoy a generous measure of health, prosperity and happiness. But so far as the great majority of the human beings who have ever lived are concerned, Humanism has the hopeless message that their sufferings are unredeemable. It is from this point of view above all that it constitutes a profoundly tragic vision of human existence.

12

The most clear-minded Humanists have always been conscious of this. Thus Bertrand Russell wrote in a well-known early essay:

> That Man is the product of causes which had no prevision of the end they were achieving; that his origin, his growth, his hopes and fears, his loves and his beliefs, are but the outcome of accidental collocations of atoms; that no fire, no heroism, no intensity of thought and feeling, can preserve an individual life beyond the grave; that all the labours of the ages, all the devotion, all the inspiration, all the noonday brightness of human genius, are destined to extinction in the vast death of the solar system, and that the whole temple of Man's achievement must inevitably be buried beneath the debris of a universe in ruins – all these things, if not quite beyond dispute, are yet so nearly certain, that no philosophy which rejects them can hope to stand. Only within the scaffolding of these truths, only on the firm foundation of unyielding despair, can the soul's habitation henceforth be safely built.[1]

Now I do not say that because this pessimistic vision of the human situation is so unwelcome it must also be false. That would be an absurd argument. Rather, I am drawing out the contrast between the Humanist and the Christian visions of human existence. Christianity sees our life in relation to a divine purpose of love, and sees that purpose as creating in and through and out of suffering a good of infinite value, a good which will be found to justify all that has been undergone on the way to it. Christianity's response to the facts of wickedness and suffering, which challenge this vision, will be discussed in chapter IV, section 1. But the claim that our human life is part of a vast creative process leading to unlimited good is so momentous that any rational person must wish to probe it. Unless he judges that such a claim cannot possibly be true – and that would be a dogmatic stance hard to justify – the Humanist should be willing to join the Christian in looking again at the centre of Christianity, which is the person of Jesus, and at the beliefs about God and about the living of life and the facing of death which have grown out of the impact of this person. The present book is offered as a help in doing that.

NOTE

1. Bertrand Russell, *Mysticism and Logic, and Other Essays*, London: Edward Arnold, 1918, pp. 47f. In 1962 Russell wrote in a letter: 'My

own outlook on the cosmos and on human life is substantially un-changed' (*Autobiography*, Vol. III, London: Allen & Unwin, and New York: Simon & Schuster, 1969, p. 173).

I   Jesus – the Centre of Christianity

1 *The challenge of Jesus*

The centre of Christianity is also its starting-point – Jesus of Nazareth. This is true both of Christianity as a whole, as a vast complex historical phenomenon spanning (so far) nineteen centuries, and also of the Christian faith of any individual in any age. It follows that Christianity is not centrally a set of beliefs or an ethic or a sacred scripture or an ecclesiastical organization. It is a response of discipleship to Jesus of Nazareth; and these other things have come about as consequences of that response. When the community of disciples reflected upon the implications of its response Christian beliefs began to be formed; when it sought to describe life within the ambience of that response the Christian ethic was being set forth (see below, pp. 61–66); in remembering the beginnings of this response it produced the New Testament; and through living in a world that was alien to it the community became moulded into an ecclesiastical organization. But the primary and central fact remains the impact of Jesus of Nazareth upon mankind – which means, ultimately, upon individual men and women.

It follows that the primary task of Christian communication is not to argue about theological ideas or about the inspiration of the Bible or the authority of the church, but to try to relay to others the impact of Jesus of Nazareth, thus making possible their own response of discipleship to him. It is a matter of communicating the Christian starting-point, and this is more a task of pointing out and proclaiming than of proving, more a matter of announcing than of arguing. For Jesus of Nazareth can in the end only be presented, through the New Testament memory of him, and responded to.

But lest this seems too individualistic a conception of Christianity, centring overmuch upon personal faith, let me show how the rational and philosophical side of religion is connected with it. The 'take it or leave it' situation applies only to the Christian starting-point. As soon as we move beyond this we are in a different realm. The starting-point is something 'given'; in traditional theological language it is revealed. But what Christians do in response to that revelation belongs to the human side of religion. The theologies they construct in their attempts to understand that revelation, and the forms of life they develop on the basis of those theologies, are fallible human works, liable to all the distorting effects of pride, egoism, jealousy, lust for power and fear of freedom and responsibility. Therefore the logical and philosophical testing of Christian belief, the moral criticism of the Christian ethic, the literary and historical investigation of the Bible, and the political, economic and psychological analysis of the churches are all very much in order. For what these disciplines are scrutinizing are the cultural content and forms of men's responses to Jesus of Nazareth. Seen in this light, these critical activities are part of the response itself. They are the necessary self-criticism of a very human community which is always liable to develop ideas, practices and institutions which in greater or lesser degree work *against* the impact of Jesus of Nazareth. For through the centuries Christian theology has produced a number of doctrines which are unchristian in that they conflict with Jesus' revelation of God's love (for example, the doctrine that God 'from before all ages' predestined some men to be saved and others to be damned); Christian morality has produced rules and attitudes which are not justifiable when tested by the spirit of Jesus (for example, the idea that birth control is sinful); the biblical writings have been endowed with a legalistic authority which is alien to their true nature; and the churches have developed into in-groups and power centres whose character hinders and distorts the influence of the Jesus whom they seek to proclaim (for example, by the class-stratification of the churches in Britain or by their racially segregated condition in the southern states of the United States of America). In all these spheres the most rigorous testing and criticism of actual Christian teachings and practices are needed in the light of the Christian starting-point. This is the Reformation principle that the church must continually struggle to purify itself in order to be more true to its Lord. In this process it may even happen that some of the external critics are doing better service to Christianity than ecclesiastical defenders of the status quo.

So there is within Christianity the fullest scope for critical thinking. But still the central fact, in relation to which all else is judged, remains the person of Jesus of Nazareth.

Jesus of Nazareth lived within the borders of what is today Israel. He was wholly and unambiguously a human being, by race a Jew, in sex a man, culturally of the first century AD. We shall turn presently (in section 3) to the language which the church began to use about him within a generation of his death, in which he was hailed as a divine being; and the further growth of this into the metaphysical doctrines of the Incarnation and the Trinity. But these belong to the developing human tradition which we call Christianity, not to the faith and teaching of Jesus himself. The original response was made by his disciples to Jesus as a man. And if we today come to share their faith we are likely to do so by first being stirred either by the qualities of the human figure or by the human meaning of his teaching.

If we had lived as Jesus' contemporaries and had met him, what would have happened? Suppose we had not only heard him from within a large crowd whom he was addressing but had met him personally, as many people must have done, at the house where he was staying during his visit to their village. I shall not attempt to describe his appearance or manner or voice and so on; for we know nothing about these. But we do know some of the sorts of things he said and did, and we know the kind of impression that he made upon a number of people. We know this from the New Testament memories about his influence, from the kinds of sayings and doings that were most vividly remembered and recorded, and from the effect on ourselves today of some of those acts and sayings.

Meeting him would in my opinion have been for most of us a profoundly disturbing experience. For we are all living in ruts, in a familiar web of personal relationships, in well established patterns of thinking and valuing, habitual ways of conducting our lives, well worn routes through the days and weeks and months and years, guided by limited but long accepted goals and ambitions. Out of our life has grown an enveloping shell which establishes us at the centre of a world within which we can function more or less effectively, and in which everything is related to ourself. This concave shape of our private world of meaning, centring upon ourselves, is a universal characteristic of human life and is identical with what traditional theology has called the fallen state of mankind (on which, however, see pp. 95–97).

Generally, the older we are the deeper is the rut in which we live. This is perhaps why Jesus said that the kingdom of heaven is open to little children and that to enter it we must become like them. For they are still universally receptive and do not have to break out of enclosed worlds of meaning in order to respond to the divine reality. But we adults have lost the innocent openness of the child. And to meet Jesus of Nazareth would be for us such a profoundly disturbing experience precisely because it would threaten the existence that we have made for ourselves. We should realize that here is someone who is going to undermine our world, the world of meaning of which we are the centre. We should even find ourselves threatened with a kind of death, the death of our present selves, and should experience in one way or another the alarm of the wealthy young man to whom Jesus said: ' "If you wish to go the whole way, go, sell your possessions, and give to the poor, and then you will have riches in heaven; and come, follow me." When the young man heard this, he went away with a heavy heart; for he was a man of great wealth' (Matt. 19.21f., NEB).[1]

But that which threatens our death also offers us life! For the quality which so disturbingly challenges us also stirs within us our true selves as we are to become in God's intention, and offers us exciting intimations of a more free and authentic existence. This quality which encounters us in Jesus is an intense awareness of people as being of value, and an utterly unselfish concern for their well-being and fulfilment. The French Roman Catholic philosopher Gabriel Marcel has called it *disponibilité*, openness and availability to others. It is to be so liberated from self-importance, so unthreatened by the otherness of others, that one can respond to them freely and immediately. In Jesus' own mind it meant seeing people as children of God to whom he was seeking to give the quality of existence which the New Testament calls eternal life. This positive unselfish goodness – the New Testament names it *agape*, love – often seems to have had a double effect upon those who met Jesus. They felt condemned by their own consciences in the light of his serene unselfishness; but they also felt attracted to the adventure of unselfishness as a positive possibility for themselves. We see this in Peter's reaction: 'Go, Lord, leave me, sinner that I am!' (Luke 5.8, NEB) – and then his faithful following of Jesus in his own life right up to a martyr's death.

The spirit of love was defined by Jesus when he spoke of the willingness to forgive unto seventy times seven, to go the second mile, to turn the other cheek, to be robbed of one's coat. Above all it was incarnated in Jesus himself: he gave himself wholly to his neighbours, the people of Galilee and Judaea in his own day, giving up the possibilities of marriage and a family, of owning property and amassing wealth, even the possibility of a normal span of life on this earth, in order to heal the sick and open to many the possibility of a new and better life.

Most of us are not called to the same basic renunciations that Jesus took upon himself. We are, however, called to embody his self-giving love within the particular circumstances of our own lives. This may involve spending ourselves in a particular work; it may involve giving large amounts of our finances to help others; it may involve great efforts, perhaps great sacrifices, in the building of better personal relationships; it may involve costly acts of forgiveness and acceptance and caring; it may involve all sorts of deliberate renunciations for the sake of others – just what it means has to be discovered by each individual for his or her self. But to be confronted even at the remove of more than nineteen centuries by the life and words of Jesus of Nazareth is – for very many people at least – to be inescapably challenged by self-giving love. We receive a piercing hint that the enclosed security which we instinctively safeguard ultimately means death rather than life, and that the self-giving to which he calls us ultimately means gain rather than loss. So Jesus said: 'Whoever cares for his own safety is lost; but if a man will let himself be lost for my sake, he will find his true self. What will a man gain by winning the whole world, at the cost of his own true self?' (Matt. 16.25f., NEB).

Psychologically this means that the valuations, the sense of the meaning of human life, the estimate of human possibilities, the conception of human sanity and wholeness embodied in Jesus of Nazareth are at variance with those embodied in ourselves. If we respond to him as the healer of our own lives this means that his values and meanings, purposes and assumptions are more convincing and attractive to us than our own, so that we want to abandon ours and adopt his. We are then in the process of dying to our old world of meaning and being born again into his; for 'unless a man has been born over again he cannot see the kingdom of God' (John 3.3, NEB).

2 *Jesus' death and resurrection*

Until recently Christian thought was accustomed to focus upon Christ's crucifixion as though it were an isolated event that could be understood by itself apart from the whole life which it climaxed. Jesus' death was seen, for example, in the earliest period as a ransom paid to the devil to redeem the souls of men; then as a satisfaction made to appease the divine honour and majesty for the wrong of man's disobedience; or again as Jesus' bearing in our place the punishment justly due for our sinfulness. According to these and other traditional theories of the atonement the death of Christ transforms man's relation to God *ex opere operato,* simply by the event itself taking place – as, for example, in human affairs the act of handing over money in payment of a debt or a fine radically alters the legal situation.

But more recently it has been realized that Christ's death has to be seen in its relation to his life in its entirety, both as arising out of what had gone before and as throwing light upon the significance of it all. In other words the meaning of Jesus' death is part of the meaning of his life.

To see why Jesus' death on the cross has always been so significant for Christians we do not need to invoke the unintelligibilities of traditional stained-glass window theology, with its bizarre notion of a divine auditing of the moral accounts, infinite punishment or infinite satisfaction being required to balance the infinite wrong of disobedience to infinite majesty. Looking at the cross as a part of history we can see that the crucifixion of Jesus expressed the violent reaction of individual and corporate selfishness to the challenge of transcendent goodness; and that in accepting this death, from which he could only have escaped by desisting from his public ministry, Jesus was accepting the claim of transcendent goodness upon him. Can Jesus be said, then, to have died on behalf of mankind? Not in any juridical sense; but in the sense that his love for his fellows, reflecting God's love for them, was strong enough for him to accept death at their hands rather than abandon his vocation to draw all who would respond into the life of God's children.

Three main human forces brought about Jesus' death: religion, in the person of the Jerusalem priesthood; ordinary human nature, in the persons of the members of the mob which howled for his crucifixion; and the powers of law and order, the state, in the persons of Pilate and the Roman army of occupation.

First, human law and order was involved through the Roman forces and their commander whose name has become part of the Christian creed – 'suffered under Pontius Pilate'. The state as such cannot be expected to recognize transcendent goodness and cannot be blamed for not doing so. But it can be expected to act justly and to refuse to be used as a tool by human envy and malice to destroy the innocent. When it does allow itself to be used as an instrument of hatred or prejudice it crucifies the defenceless, the vulnerable, the underprivileged, the disenfranchised, among whom was once Jesus, born in a stable without wealth or power or status or vote. When the state adopts a policy of exterminating the Jews in Nazi Germany; or of racial apartheid in South Africa; or of racial discrimination in some of the southern states of the United States of America; or of long continued neglect to develop dependent territories as was the case in much of the British empire; or in the bombing of North Vietnam – in all such cases in their varying degrees states are working against the purpose of God as this was seen at work on earth in the life of Jesus of Nazareth. There is a moral continuity between the judicial murder of Jesus and immoral policies pursued by states throughout history and today: 'Inasmuch as you have done it unto the least of these my brethren you have done it unto me' (Matt. 25.40, RSV).[2]

But just because the crucifixion of Jesus lies morally on the same plane as all other occasions when the forces of law and order have become instruments of injustice, that crucifixion has also become a force working on the plane of history against such injustices. For the light by which we see these policies to be unjust and by which we find them morally intolerable is the light of Christ slowly penetrating the public conscience. It is this that has at least begun to open the eyes and quicken the moral sense of Christendom. And at this point the right response to the cross of Christ must be a quickened conscience expressing itself in political terms.

The second force that sent Jesus to his death was ordinary human nature represented by the Jerusalem mob made up no doubt partly of Jerusalem citizens and partly of Galilean and other pilgrims there for the Passover. They were of course worked upon and misled by agitators. But they allowed themselves to be misled. Their bloodlust was aroused; ugly and sadistic impulses swirled to the surface and took charge, so that the mob yelled, 'Crucify him, crucify him!' What is evil here, of course, is not the fact of having such destructive impulses within one – for they are part of the complex structure of our human nature – but becoming dominated and ruled by them. And what so profoundly antagonized some of Jesus' contemporaries during the two or three years of his public ministry, so that in the end in the intense electric atmosphere of that Passover at Jerusalem hatred boiled over into raging violence, was the moral judgment and claim and challenge inherent in the presence of outstanding human goodness. As a bright light creates shadows that would not otherwise be there, so luminous moral integrity and single-minded unselfishness shows up our own narrow and selfish hearts. There is nothing so disturbing as genuine moral – that is to say, human – excellence in another because it lays an inescapable demand upon ourselves, a demand so manifest that it does not even need to be spoken. In some situation in which there is dangerous work to be done for the common safety, when someone steps forward and volunteers to be one of those who do it, everyone else feels 'put on the spot' and challenged to follow suit. This is how we are made. And Jesus' very presence constituted an implicit challenge and claim, the challenge that unselfishness constitutes for the selfish; that courage constitutes for the cowardly; that a dedicated and disciplined life constitutes for the slack and aimless. But above all it was the challenge of one who was living consciously in the presence of God. This challenge is so sharp that in the end one has either to respond in faith with one's whole being or else utterly reject the bearer of the challenge. And the death of Christ clamoured for by an ordinary crowd of people was that rejection, a rejection with which if we are entirely honest we must all to some extent identify ourselves.

And yet the result of that death has been that God's claim upon us has only been intensified. For to reject a challenge is to recognize it *as* a challenge and so to be all the more challenged by it. So through the centuries the cross of Christ has become a turning point towards faith in the experience of millions.

And then the third force that brought about Jesus' death was religion. The planning and much of the motivation and driving zeal behind the operation came from within the Sanhedrin, the ruling council of Jerusalem's religious hierarchy. They could not stand Jesus' message of the immediate presence of God as unlimitedly gracious and unlimitedly demanding love. For it spelt the death of religion, if we mean by religion the human organizing of the God-man relationship. The priestly religion of Jerusalem with which Jesus clashed was a highly developed and professional organizing of this relationship, channelling it within an elaborate network of sacred laws and customs. And if those laws really were sacred, then Jesus was anti-sacred and blasphemous in living and teaching a direct relationship to God with practical implications spreading out over the whole of life, far beyond the narrow ecclesiastical channels.

But once again, Jesus' life, and the final stark revelation in his death of the meaning of his life, have changed our religious situation. The priestly mind may still try to confine God within churches, creeds and sacraments and try to hedge his love within a framework of ecclesiastical authority. But the reality inevitably breaks forth again and again.

I have referred very little so far to the resurrection of Jesus. Nevertheless it has been in the background of all that has been said. For the entire Christian understanding of Jesus' life and death represents the point of view of the community that was created by the experience of his resurrection. That is to say, but for this mysterious event which dominated and coloured the thinking of the first generation of believers, Christianity would never have been more than a dying memory of a dead prophet. But the early Christian preaching as we hear it echoed in the Acts of the Apostles and the Letters of St Paul was never about a dead teacher or healer or prophet or even Messiah. It was always about Jesus, who had been raised by God from the dead and who was thereby known to be indeed his chosen agent. What gave force to their preaching was their ability to say, 'The Jesus we speak of has been raised by God, as we can all bear witness' (Acts 2.32, NEB). They testified that after his execution Jesus had appeared to his closest disciples, spoken with them, renewed and confirmed their faith in him and raised it to a new pitch, so that they now saw him not only as their own beloved teacher but as Messiah, the man in whom God was at work redeeming his world. This certainty that Jesus had been raised and thereby revealed as the Christ runs right through the New Testament. It is not only the explicit basis of the early church's missionary activity as this is documented in Acts and the Letters. It also affects the gospel accounts of Jesus' life prior to his death and resurrection; for the gospel writers and those who had successively transmitted the material to them could not help sometimes thinking of the earthly Jesus in terms of his ascended glory, reading back (as St John in particular does) his resurrected majesty into his earthly life.

24

It is now very difficult to be sure of the precise character of the event which we call the resurrection. It is presented in the gospels as a bodily event – the crucified body of Jesus came back to life, leaving behind it an empty tomb, and was seen, heard and perhaps touched by some of his disciples. But there are also curious counter indications within the gospels. The resurrected Jesus suddenly appears inside a locked room in Jerusalem; he vanishes into thin air at the inn on the Emmaus road; he is not recognized by some of his followers; and there is the strange statement about an appearance in Galilee: 'And when they saw him they worshipped him; but some doubted' (Matt. 28.17, RSV). It also appears on closer examinations of the texts that there are two different strands of tradition, one of appearances in Galilee and other in Jerusalem, which cannot easily be harmonized together. Furthermore, there is evidence that the crucial story of the empty tomb does not belong to the earliest phase of Christian preacing. For it does not occur in St Paul's references to the resurrection in I Corinthians 15, a document which enables us to glimpse the developing tradition at a stage prior to that enshrined in the gospels.

On the other hand, one asks oneself how at the Feast of Pentecost, only forty days after Jesus' crucifixion, the apostles could publicly preach the resurrection in Jerusalem if in fact Jesus' body was lying mouldering in a tomb a few hundred yards away. Why did it not occur to anyone to check their story? To this, scholars on the other side of the debate reply that the whole account of Joseph of Arimathaea's garden tomb is part of the legend of the bodily resurrection and that in all probability Jesus' body was thrown into a common criminals' grave.

It appears to me that we shall never know with any certainty whether the resurrection of Jesus was a bodily event; or consisted in visions (technically hallucinations, perhaps auditory as well as visual) of Jesus, or in an intense sense of his unseen personal presence. The fairly strong probability seems to me to be that it was a matter of visions. But whatever it was, we do know something of its effects. The main result was the transformation of a forlorn handful of former followers of an executed and discredited prophet into a coherent and dynamic fellowship with a faith which determined its life and enabled it to convince, to grow, to survive persecution and become the dominant religion of the Roman Empire. In the days after Jesus' crucifixion something momentous happened to bring the disciples' faith back to life, and indeed to more than its former life; and according to the accounts of the Christian community itself that momentous event was the resurrection of Jesus to a life that was mysteriously more than his former life. He was present now in such a way that they could no longer doubt his lordship. And so his resurrection became the foundation of their faith.[3]

3   Was Jesus unique?

What do we mean when we speak of the uniqueness of Jesus? Strictly, that someone is unique simply means that there is only one of him. But of course in this sense everyone is unique. And so the expression, as it has been used by the church, must be meant as shorthand for something more. Generally, when the phrase is used as a kind of verbal flag which we are being expected to salute, it stands for the notion that Jesus was the unique Son of God and is as such the sole doorway to salvation, the one and only point of saving contact between God and man, so that sooner or later all men must, if they are to come to God, find him and respond to him in the person of Jesus Christ.

We shall be looking in more detail later (chapter IV) at the whole question of the relation between Christianity and the other religions of the world. But at this point we want to look, reverently but honestly, at the traditional doctrine of the Incarnation, according to which Jesus was nothing less than God become man – or, more precisely, that he was God the Son, the Second Person of the Holy Trinity, living a human life. This conception is deeply engrained in the hallowed imagery of Christian devotion, and the language which carries it has become the traditional and orthodox language of the Christian church. The question that is being raised today in many quarters concerns not so much the use

26

of this language as its meaning. Is it to be understood literally, or as some kind of poetic diction? Was Jesus metaphorically, or non-metaphorically (i.e. literally), the 'Son of God'; and if the latter, what does it mean to say that he was literally the Son of God?

Let us begin with the religious reality to which I have pointed as the centre of Christianity, namely the historical Jesus in his relationship to God as the heavenly Father.

He was a man marvellously open to God, living consciously in the divine presence and responsively to the divine purpose. Out of his intense God-consciousness he was able to speak with certainty about the heavenly Father, to convey the challenge of God's will and to declare God's judgment and forgiveness; and the divine power of life flowed through his hands in physical healing. The intense sense of God's reality expressed in Jesus' life and words was infectious, so that in his presence men and women either joined him in a gloriously liberating surrender to God, or reacted violently against the man who had made God real to them. Undoubtedly, in the world which he knew Jesus lived in a closer awareness of God and a more total obedience to God than anyone else, so that it was natural for him to call men to become his disciples. And it was equally natural for them to follow him as their Lord and to preach his message to others. It was natural again that after his death and Easter appearances his disciples, filled with his spirit, should proclaim Jesus as Lord and Saviour to all who should respond to him. And those to whom God thus became real and present through Jesus received new life, new purpose, and a new spirit of mutual love. They were redeemed from the old existence and entered into a new and higher quality of life, the eternal life of fellowship with God.

Now it used to be assumed – and in some Christian circles it still is assumed – that this Jesus, who lived in Palestine in the first third of the first century AD, was conscious of being God incarnate, and taught that he was God incarnate, so that you must either believe him or reject him as a deceiver or a megalomaniac. 'Mad, bad, or God' went the argument. And of course if Jesus did indeed claim to be God incarnate, then this dilemma, or trilemma, does arise. But did he claim this? The assumption that he did is largely based on the Fourth Gospel, for it is here that Jesus makes precisely such claims. He says 'I and the Father are one', 'No one comes to the Father, but by me' and 'He who has seen me has seen the Father'.[4] But it is no secret today, after more than a hundred years of the scholarly study of the scriptures, that very few New Testament experts now hold that the Jesus who actually lived ever spoke those words, or their Aramaic equivalents. They are much more probably words put into his mouth by a Christian writer who is expressing the view of Christ which had been arrived at in his part of the church, probably two or three generations after Jesus's death.[5] And it is likewise doubted whether the few sayings of the same kind in the other gospels are authentic words of Jesus.[6]

How, then, did this Christian deification of Jesus – which began within the first decades after his death and was essentially completed by the end of the first century – take place? Such a development is not as hard to understand in the ancient world as it would be today. The starting-point, as we have seen, was a great charismatic prophet and healer who was so obediently responsive to God that he made God real to others as their heavenly Father. In his presence men and women were born again into the kingdom which is God's rule in human life. After his death there were visions of him which overcame his death in the minds of his disciples and sent them out to preach Jesus as their living Lord. At this point the need must have become acute for publicly intelligible titles by which to identify Jesus to their hearers; and as the first hearers, like the first preachers, were all Jews, the inevitable title was that of the Messiah (in Greek *Christos*), God's agent sent at the end of the present evil age to inaugurate the holy kingdom. But this was not yet deification: 'As Messiah, Jesus was not a supernatural being, but a man with a particular status.'[7] The further title that came to be used, either independently of 'Messiah' or growing out of it, was 'son of God'. This term had roots both in the surrounding Hellenistic world and also within Judaism itself. In the ancient Near East it was not uncommon for a great man to be described as a son of God. To quote Cullman's summary, 'The origin of the "son of God" concept lies in ancient oriental religions, in which above all kings were thought to be begotten of gods . . . In the New Testament period also the Roman emperors were entitled *divi filius* [son of the/a god]. But in Hellenism the expression is by no means limited to rulers. Anyone believed to possess some kind of divine power was called "son of God" by others, or gave himself the title. All miracle workers were "sons of God", or, as one also said, *theioi andres* [divine men]: Apollonius of Tyana, for instance, whose life is described by Philostratus in a form which is often reminiscent of our Gospels; or Alexander of Abonoteichus, whom we know through Lucian. Used in this sense, the title was quite common. In the New Testament period one could meet everywhere men who called themselves "sons of God" because of their peculiar vocation or miraculous powers.'[8] And within Judaism, 'In the Old Testament we find this expression used in three ways: the whole people of Israel is called "son of God"; kings bear the title; persons with a special commission from God, such as angels, and perhaps also the Messiah, are so called.'[9] In particular, the ancient Hebrew kings became 'son of God' by divine adoption – 'You are my son, today I have begotten you' (Ps. 2.7, RSV); 'I will be his father, and he shall be my son' (II Sam. 7.14, RSV). Jesus was believed, as Messiah, to be of the royal line of David and true king of Israel, and this may well explain the use of a conflation of Old Testament quotations in the story of his baptism, 'Thou are my beloved Son; with thee I am well pleased.'[10]

Whether the son of God title entered the language of the church from Hebraic or Hellenistic sources, or indeed from both, continues to be disputed. But wherever this language came from, the Roman Catholic theologian Hans Küng accurately summarizes contemporary research concerning the historical Jesus when he says that 'even more conservative exegetes conclude that Jesus himself did not assume any title implying messianic dignity: not "Messiah", nor "Son of David", nor "Son", nor "Son of God" '.[11]

But if the historical Jesus did not think of himself as divine, or lay claim to a divine status, may it not nevertheless have been proper for the church to have affirmed Jesus' divinity after his resurrection? Does not this event single him out as utterly unique, not only for Christians but in relation to the whole world and the whole of history?

I think we can indeed say (as was implied in the previous section) that it was the resurrection experience – whatever form this may have taken – that launched the Christian movement, including its search for titles with which to identify Jesus; and to this extent it is true that the description of Jesus as Son of God is a product, and in that cultural milieu probably an almost inevitable product, of the resurrection. We who are Christians today inherit the language in which the post-resurrection church came to speak about the Lord; and it is the proper meaning of this language that is now under discussion. But if it is suggested that we are required by Jesus' resurrection to adopt a literal interpretation of incarnational language, the answer must I think be that this is to go beyond what the resurrection experience of the first disciples either requires or authorizes.

We have seen that the resurrection event may have consisted either in the seeing of a vision or visions of Jesus in resplendent glory, or – less probably – in the physical emergence of his revivified body from the tomb. If it were the former, visions of the dead do not necessarily establish the divinity of those appearing in this way. (Nor are visions of great religious figures unique to Christianity.[12]) Neither, in the world of the writers and the first readers of the New Testament, did a physical resurrection. In the late biblical thought-world the notion of the dead coming bodily back to life was not so startling or contrary to accepted possibilities as it seems today. The Letter to the Hebrews says that in olden times 'Women received their dead by resurrection' (11.35, RSV). Jesus himself is reported as raising Lazarus, Jairus' daughter, and a widow's son, and as having told John the Baptist's messengers to tell him that they had seen that the dead were being raised. And Matthew records that at the time of Jesus' death 'the tombs also were opened, and many bodies of the saints who had fallen asleep were raised, and coming out of the tombs after his resurrection they went into the holy city and appeared to many' (27.52, RSV).

Thus the physical raising of the dead was evidently an accepted possibility at that time; and by the same token a resurrection story cannot have seemed quite so uniquely earth-shaking as it does today. Thus it need not astonish us that the first Christian preachers, proclaiming Jesus' resurrection, did not draw the conclusion that he was God but that he was a man chosen by God for a special work and declared by his resurrection to be the Messiah and Lord (Acts 2.22 and 36).

We have seen that someone identified as Messiah might have attracted the title son of God, as indeed might a Palestinian miracle-worker. But this title, whether applied to ancient Hebrew kings or to charismatic figures in the Hellenistic world, was metaphorical and honorific in its use rather than literally descriptive. And no doubt Jesus himself spoke in this same poetic way of God as our Father and men as his sons. But in the course of time, as the Latin theologians got to work, the symbolism hardened into dogma, and the metaphorical son of God became the metaphysical God the Son, Second Person of the eternal Trinity. This development reached its completion at the Council of Chalcedon (AD 451) in the dogma that Jesus had two natures, human and divine, being 'of one substance with the Father as regards his Godhead, and at the same time of one substance with us as regards his manhood', and thus 'in two natures, without confusion, without change, without division, without separation; the distinction of natures being in no way annulled by the union, but with the characteristics of each nature being preserved and coming together to form one person and subsistence . . .'. But how one person can be both eternal and yet born in time; omnipotent and yet with the limited capacity of a human being; omniscient and yet with finite human knowledge; omnipresent and yet confined to one region of space at a time; how, in short, the same person can have the full attributes of both God and man – has never been explained, and seems indeed to be on a par with the statement that a figure drawn on paper has the attributes of both a circle and a square.

The very natural questioning of this development does not however mean that Jesus is not the Lord and Saviour whom we experience him as being, or that the Son-of-God language which the church has developed should be abandoned.

It means rather that to call Jesus God, Son of God, God incarnate, etc. is to use poetic (or if you like 'mythological') language which appropriately expresses loving devotion and commitment, but which is misused when it is treated as a set of literal propositions from which to draw further literal conclusions. That the imagery of incarnation lacks any non-metaphorical meaning was made clear by the history of the christological heresies, most of which were misguided attempts to give literal content to the idea of incarnation instead of leaving it in the realm of mystery and religious myth. That Jesus is my Lord and Saviour is language like that of the lover for whom his Helen is the sweetest girl in the world. Logically, there can only be one sweetest girl in the world; but if we treat the lover's words literally and infer from them the claim that every other girl in the world is less sweet than Helen, we shall not be doing justice to the kind of language he is using. And likewise if from the confession of Jesus as Lord and Saviour we infer that men cannot respond to God except through Jesus, we misuse the language of personal commitment and turn living religion into dogmatic exclusiveness.[13] We shall thus be continuing with this same topic when we come (in chapter IV) to the question of the Christian attitude to the other world religions.

NOTES

1. NEB: The New English Bible.
2. RSV: American Revised Standard Version.
3. For a discussion in dialogue form of different points of view concerning the character of the resurrection event, see Geoffrey Lampe and Donald MacKinnon, *The Resurrection* (London: Mowbray, and Philadelphia: Westminster Press, 1967). An important recent challenging book on the resurrection is Willi Marxsen, *The Resurrection of Jesus of Nazareth* (ET, London: SCM Press, and Philadelphia: Fortress Press, 1970).
4. John 10.30; 14.6; 14.9 (RSV).
5. See e.g. Ernst Käsemann, *The Testament of Jesus*, ET, London: SCM Press, and Philadelphia: Fortress Press, 1968, chapter 2.
6. Cf. Hans Conzelmann, *An Outline of the Theology of the New Testament*, 2nd ed., ET, London: SCM Press, and New York: Harper & Row, 1969, p. 127, referring to Matt. 11.27, Luke 10.22 and Mark 13.32.
7. Conzelmann, p. 77.

8. Oscar Cullmann, *The Christology of the New Testament*, ET, London: SCM Press, and Philadelphia: Westminster Press, 2nd ed., 1963, pp. 271f.

9. Cullmann, pp. 272f.

10. Mark 1.11, RSV (cf. Matt. 3.17; Luke 3.22). Cf. Joachim Jeremias, *New Testament Theology* I, ET, London: SCM Press, and New York: Scribner's, 1971, pp. 53f.

11. Hans Küng, *On Being a Christian*, ET, New York: Doubleday, 1976, and London: Collins, 1977, p. 289. Cf. Wolfhart Pannenberg, 'Today it must be taken as all but certain that the pre-Easter Jesus neither designated himself as Messiah (or Son of God) nor accepted such a confession to him from others' (*Jesus – God and Man*, ET, London: SCM Press, and Philadelphia: Westminster Press, 1968, p. 327). It should be noted that both of these writers, together, probably, with most of the New Testament scholars whom they are citing, believe the traditional doctrine of the Incarnation; but they do not claim that Jesus himself believed or taught it.

12. There are several detailed accounts of nineteenth- and twentieth-century resurrection appearances of Hindu gurus in Yogananda Paramahansa, *Autobiography of a Yogi* (Los Angeles: Self-Realization Fellowship 1971, 12th ed., 1981).

13. For a further development of the ideas in this section see *The Myth of God Incarnate*, ed. John Hick (London: SCM Press, 1977, and Philadelphia: Westminster Press, 1978).

II The God whom Jesus Worshipped

1 God as transcendent personal mind

There are undoubtedly many aspects of Christianity as it has developed through the centuries that we can leave aside. But it seems to me that we cannot, if we are to respond realistically to Jesus of Nazareth, leave aside the God in whom he believed. We do not deal honestly with Jesus of Nazareth if we ignore what was to him the most real of all realities. For he was so completely free within himself and available to others precisely because he was so completely dedicated to his heavenly Father's work. It is impossible, in the remembered teaching of Jesus, to separate what he said about human life from what he said about God. He did not, for example, say 'Love your neighbours', but 'Love the Lord your God with all your heart, with all your soul, with all your strength, and with all your mind; and your neighbour as yourself' (Luke 10.27, NEB). And he did not say 'Love your enemies'; but 'Love your enemies and pray for your persecutors; only so can you be children of your heavenly Father, who makes his sun rise on good and bad alike and sends the rain on the honest and the dishonest' (Matt. 5.44f., NEB). Everything was for him within the context of God's presence and purpose. It was because God knows and cares for us that we can ourselves be freed from self-concern and enabled to live without anxiety. It is because God is love that we can also live by love; because God has forgiven us that we can afford to forgive others. For the way of self-giving love is the way anyone tends to live when he is conscious of being known, forgiven and valued by God.

Accordingly, Jesus of Nazareth lived his life in conscious dependence upon God. He spent long periods in prayer to his heavenly Father. He always described himself as God's agent, and perhaps he saw his life in the light of Old Testament prophecies concerning God's suffering servant who was to give his life for his fellows. In short, God was so completely real to him that it is impossible to think of him without this consciousness of God.

But who is this 'God' in relation to whom Jesus continually lived? We must go on from Jesus of Nazareth to the God in whom he believed.

God is dead – so Nietzsche asserted a century ago and so many proclaim today. Needless to say this cannot be a fact about God (for if he was alive at any time he is alive at all times) but about our idea of him. God's death is a cultural event: the idea of deity has faded and died in men's minds. Our typical attitude to God today is like our attitude to some venerable figure of the distant past who is still spoken of with respect but who has long since ceased to be relevant to our practical affairs.

Because God is dead in the modern mind we have to make a positive effort to think about him. The imagination has to break out of its ordinary paths in order to entertain such an utterly strange possibility. And Christian communication must therefore have recourse to the arts in which the imagination is awakened and stretched and made open to new possibilities. A great deal of modern art serves this function, but instead of using the work of any of the great artists of our time I propose to draw upon a new form of popular literature in which intellectual speculation is quite explicit and on the surface – science fiction.

The Black Cloud by Fred Hoyle (who was a professor of astronomy at Cambridge University) introduces ideas that can begin to enlarge the imagination in the direction of the idea of God.

Hoyle describes a cosmic brain, millions of times larger and more complex than a human brain. This cosmic brain is not, like ours, tightly bunched inside a skull, so that its possibilities of development are rigidly limited. It is instead widely spread out in space on the surfaces of floating pieces of frozen matter held together in an electromagnetic field and forming a gaseous cloud hundreds of millions of miles across. This gigantic brain can add new cells to itself as

35

required so that an old cloud – and the one which in the novel replenishes its energies from our sun is some five hundred million years old – is larger than a young one. (Old clouds produce new ones from time to time by bedding out some of their own cells to form a fresh nucleus.)

The Cloud is surprised to find what is to it a very rudimentary form of intelligence on our planet, and quickly absorbs all the information about human life that can be transmitted to it. It addresses the group of scientists who are in communication with it, using human language put at its disposal by a computer controlled by radio impulses. Shortly before the Cloud moves off again into outer space it speaks of what it calls 'the deep problems'.

The Cloud says:

> Probably you have wondered whether a larger-scale intelligence than your own exists. Now you know that it does. In a like fashion I ponder on the existence of a larger-scale intelligence than myself. There is none within the Galaxy, and none within other galaxies so far as I am yet aware. Yet there is strong evidence, I feel, that such an intelligence does play an overwhelming part in our existence. Otherwise how is it decided how matter shall behave? How are your laws of physics determined? Why these laws and no others? These problems are of outstanding difficulty, so difficult that I have not been able to solve them. What is clear however is that such an intelligence, if it exists, cannot be spatially or temporarily limited in any way.[1]

Thus we are presented with the thought of a super-mind as far beyond our own in intellectual capacity as the human mind is beyond that of an ape or a cat. And there is the further hint of a yet greater mind, spatially and temporally unlimited, which is responsible for the basic order of the universe. One must not on this account attribute to Fred Hoyle a belief in God, for he has in other writings (particularly the last chapter of *The Nature of the Universe*) clearly repudiated any such belief. Nevertheless this novel begins to stretch the imagination in the direction in which it must go if it is to form the idea of God, and I invoke it to this end. What we have to do, if we are to grasp the concept of God, is to go yet further in the direction hinted at by the Cloud.

The first step is the very big one of conceiving of an intelligence which does not depend for its functioning upon cells of living matter and their electro-chemical changes. If we can entertain the idea of a consciousness – say, our own – surviving the dissolution of its body, we can perhaps also entertain the idea of a cosmic consciousness which has never functioned through a body at all. Its intellectual operations are purely mental and have no physical concomitants. Fundamental philosophical issues, which I cannot attempt to discuss within the plan of this book, are of course raised by such a thought. I can only list below some works in which the intelligibility of the idea of a mind not dependent upon matter is discussed.[2]

Continuing to move towards the idea of God, we have to think of a cosmic mind whose capacity is not merely enormous in comparison with our own but actually unlimited. That is to say, there is and can be nothing in relation to which its knowledge is exhausted or its comprehension baffled. It knows directly and completely every molecule, every impulse of energy, every causal connection, every thought and emotion. It is not quite correct to say that the divine knowledge and understanding are *infinite*; for knowledge and understanding must be *of* something, and if the knowable universe is finite (even though without boundaries) then so will be any knowledge and comprehension of it. Therefore God's unlimitedness as a knowing and comprehending mind is better defined as the complete adequacy of his knowledge and understanding to the knowable.

Furthermore, we have to conceive of a mind which is not temporally limited. Its consciousness is not restricted, as ours is, to successive thin cross-sections of space-time. Instead it is aware of the entirety of space-time as an undivided whole, so that the moments of which we are serially aware are all co-present to the unlimited consciousness; though it is also of course aware of temporality and all that this involves through its awareness of our own temporal experience.

God's temporal unlimitedness or eternity means that from his own point of view he simply and non-temporally *is*, while from our point of view he exists without having ever had a beginning or being liable in the future to end. Clearly, the existence of such a being cannot be dependent upon any external power: God exists in a uniquely complete and unconditioned sense.

In pictorial terms we may say that God stands outside the universe. But speaking more strictly, a mind which is not associated with a particular physical brain does not have a spatial location and so cannot properly be said to be either inside or outside the universe. It is therefore better to say that God transcends space-time, meaning by this that his knowing of it is not an event within it.

Our next step must be to the idea of God as the Creator of everything that exists other than himself. That is to say, the universe exists because God wants it to exist and would not exist if he ceased to want it to exist. It is thus absolutely dependent upon him. We shall return to the idea of creation considered in relation to modern science (see pp. 95f.); but its positive religious meaning is that God has established and structured the universe (including ourselves as part of it) to fulfil his own purposes for it; from which it follows that we shall most satisfactorily inhabit it when we live in it in accordance with those purposes.

God's power in relation to his creation (or his 'omnipotence') is then equivalent to the two circumstances that it exists by his will and that it is destined by his purposes, built into its nature, to fulfil his ends.

This reference to divine purposes brings us to a further range of aspects of the Christian idea of God. We have said so far that God is unlimited and all-knowing Mind, without beginning or end, upon whose creativity the physical universe depends for its existence and for its structure. These are unique characteristics which do not correspond to anything in ourselves. Instead of having independent and eternal existence we are limited and dependent beings. Instead of having absolute knowledge, we always know from a particular perspective within space-time. And we cannot create in the sense of bringing into existence out of nothing. But there are other aspects of God which do correspond to qualities in ourselves – above all personality, goodness, love and purpose. Of course these words have originally been developed to refer to qualities of our own human nature, and therefore they cannot apply literally to the divine Mind in its unique infinite being. It is when God's activity impinges upon our human lives that we must and properly may describe in human language his nature so disclosed to us. We speak about God's character, as we also speak about a man's, on the basis of his actions. And out of an experience of God's dealings with mankind over many centuries, and above all in the climactic few years of the life of Jesus of Nazareth, the Jewish–Christian tradition has come to know God as personal and loving, purposive and good – not that these finite terms are adequate to the infinite being of God, but that they serve, however, to describe the character of his activity in relation to our finite human life.

All these personal qualities of the infinite Mind are concentrated in the activity of love. But 'love' is a many-coloured word; of what kind is the love of God? The Christian answer points to the love for men and women that Jesus both taught and lived out in his own life.

In trying to describe this love, let us compare it with the kind that is most familiar to us, the love based upon sexual attraction, the love between a man and a woman on which marriage is based. This is an exceedingly precious and wonderful thing and one of the greatest sources of human happiness, and to distinguish it from love (*agape*) in the special New Testament sense is not in any way to disparage sexual love. But sexual love is a biologically specialized form of a more general and unrestricted attitude; and it is this latter that dimly reflects God's attitude to mankind. One of the most eminent philosophers of our time who was also one of our most distinguished atheists, Bertrand Russell, has said that despite all the complexities of the world's problems our most urgent need is not for any new invention or technique but for something simpler. He writes, 'The root of the matter is a very simple and old-fashioned thing, a thing so simple that I am ashamed to mention it, for fear of the derisive smile with which wise cynics will greet my words. The thing I mean – please forgive me for mentioning it – is love, Christian love, or compassion.'[3]

Now what Bertrand Russell called Christian love here, and what the New Testament calls by the Greek word *agape*, differs from sexual love in two ways. First, Christian love is not biologically specialized and is not specifically directed towards the opposite sex. Nor indeed is it restricted in any other way – neither to those of the same community as ourselves, nor to members of the same nation or race, nor of the same cultural or political outlook. It knows no boundaries of any kind. Its sphere is the whole realm of our relationships with other people, both direct and indirect – both our relationships with those we meet face to face and our relationships with those (the great majority of mankind) whom we never meet but whose lives are inextricably linked with our own in this embarrassingly small world. For in these days when death can be dispatched through the stratosphere at supersonic speeds, and when the economy of the whole world forms a single mesh of cause and effect, peoples at the other end of the earth are our neighbours in the biblical sense of being those to whom our actions inevitably show or fail to show caring love.

And second, Christian love is not, like sexual love, a desiring love evoked by and dependent upon the desirableness of its object. He loves her *because* she is pretty, attractive, charming. She loves him *because* he is handsome, manly, clever. And indeed beyond the sphere of sex, human love (for example, between parents and children) and human friendship is always a response to special qualities or attributes. Parents love their children because they are *their* children. Friendships are based upon such affinities as common interests and common experiences. Christian love on the other hand is not evoked by and therefore not limited to the humanly lovable. It is unconditional in its nature and universal in its range. It is a giving love, going out to people not because they have any special characteristics or qualifications but simply because they are *there*, because they are persons, neighbours under God.

We see this attitude most clearly in Jesus of Nazareth. He seems to have given himself wholly to his neighbours. He spent his life bringing a new quality of life to others, a new wholeness to the mind and healing to the body, a release from anxious preoccupations with oneself and a new openness to the neighbour. People crowded around him wherever he went, recognizing in him the power of a higher quality of life and seeking to receive it for themselves. There was evidently something very striking about him and about what he said and did that revealed a superabundant inner life by which others might be enriched. And he poured out this superabundant inner life unstintingly in healing and renewal, eventually dying a violent death rather than either limit the scope of his love or deny its meaning for human life. It is above all in Jesus that Christian faith sees love at work on earth. And so the figure of Jesus gives meaning to the statement, 'God is love (*agape*).'

There is a further aspect of the Christian idea of God that arises directly out of the divine love and that must be brought into view if our picture is not to be seriously one-sided. God has always been encountered in religious experience as absolute and unconditional demand as well as gracious loving-kindness. This element of demand arises inevitably from the very nature of love. Parents who love their children with any degree of unselfish goodness and wisdom are bound to want them to become the very best that they are capable of becoming. Thus love carries with it a moral *demand* which is the more inexorable the greater the love. And the love of God for his human children involves a claim upon us to strive towards the human perfection for which he has made us. His love for us is his active seeking of our deepest good and happiness; and this comes to us both as a judgment upon the shallow goods and narrow happinesses to which we so short-sightedly cling, and as a persistent challenging summons to adventure beyond them. To become conscious of God is automatically to be judged by the almost blinding contrast between our own self-centredness and God's perfect, because universal, love; but it is also to have opened before us the possibility of a new and better life and to hear ourselves called forward into that life.

We see and feel all this most directly when we confront Jesus of Nazareth as he is reflected in the New Testament writings. On the one hand his very existence, as one who gave himself wholly to others, was a standing condemnation of selfishness, greed and self-enclosed blindness to one's neighbours. Indeed it was because his very existence condemned them that people who supposed that they were good, particularly the scribes and Pharisees of his time, reacted so violently and eventually engineered Jesus' death.

But on the other hand people who knew that they were not good were often able to recognize his absolute goodness and respond to him. And in doing so they found that his attitude towards them was not one of condemnation but of acceptance. The obsession with guilt and expiation which has pre-occupied so much of Christian theology was not shared by Jesus and should not be projected upon his heavenly Father. Jesus accepted everyone, including prostitutes and swindlers, who could see themselves as they really were and so could recognize the better life to which he called them. This seeing and being attracted by the new and better possibility, which Jesus has revealed by himself living it, is salvation.

2 *Faith as a mode of knowledge*

The debate between sceptics and believers centres upon the question whether religious faith is veridical or illusory. But before this can usefully be discussed there has to be agreement about what it is that we are calling faith. In other words we need an agreed description of faith which will deliberately leave open the crucial question whether it is a form of self-delusion or a supremely important mode of knowledge.

It seems to me that the issue has often been obscured because the standard accounts of the nature of faith put forward by theologians, and used by sceptics as a basis for criticism, are seriously inadequate. They make the mistake of describing faith in various secondary and weakened forms instead of in its strongest and normative manifestations. This is like trying to discover the nature of gold by analysing a fivepenny tin ring covered with gilt paint instead of a twenty-four-carat solid gold bar.

Where do we find religious faith in its purest twenty-four-carat form? Surely, not in wavering half-belief or in a second-hand faith based on someone else's authority, but in the faith of saints and prophets, apostles and martyrs, God-oriented souls past and present in whose lives religious faith has been a major determining factor.

Some of the Old Testament prophets are excellent examples. One can ask what sort of state or act their faith was and then make this central to one's description of faith. In turning to the prophets then I am not now asking whether their faith was veridical but am trying to describe their distinctive religious state as this is reflected in the biblical writings. And the outstanding fact is that they acted and spoke as men who were vividly conscious of being in the presence of God. Their lives were dominated by this consciousness. Trying to stand imaginatively in their shoes, we must say that they experienced God as awesome personal power confronting them and drawing them into the sphere of his ongoing purpose. God was known to them as a dynamic will interacting with their own wills; a sheer given reality, as inescapably to be reckoned with as destructive storm and life-giving sunshine or the fixed features of the land or the hatred of their enemies and the friendship of their neighbours. He was not to them an inferred entity but an experienced reality. They were (sometimes, though doubtless not at all times) as vividly aware of being in his presence as they were of living in a material environment. Their words resound and vibrate with the sense of God's presence as a building might resound and vibrate from the tread of some great being walking through it. And the state of mind which lies behind these remarkable writings is religious faith in one of its purest forms.

In relation to this standard, the accepted theories show their inadequacy. Let us examine the two most widely held of these theories. Thomas Aquinas' view of faith has not only been official teaching until recently within the Roman Catholic communion, but its essential features have also been evident in the past within a great deal of Protestant theology. According to this Thomist view faith consists in believing religious truths because they have been divinely revealed. We believe some propositions because we can see or prove them to be true, and in these cases we have knowledge. But there are others which we cannot see or prove to be true, because they exceed the scope of our human comprehension, but which we are nevertheless invited to believe on divine authority. They are said to have been revealed through the church or in the Bible and our believing of them is faith.

Now this scholastic conception of faith does not fit the

43

biblical reality. In the faith of the prophets there was indeed an element of propositional belief, namely, believing what God said to them. But when the Old Testament is read in the light of modern biblical criticism one finds that this element is not nearly as prominent as it at first appears. For when it is said that God spoke to the prophets, this probably does not mean that they heard a voice uttering Hebrew words and sentences, but that by their insight into the human situations in which they were, and into men's motives, and above all into God's absolute righteousness and infinite mercy, they became overwhelmingly conscious of a divine command for Israel, which they expressed under an urgent sense of mission with the formula 'Thus saith the Lord . . .'. But while their faith expressed itself in this way in assertions and commands it consisted more fundamentally in their vivid compelling sense of the reality and personal presence and activity of God. And this is very remote from the Thomist conception of faith as believing theological propositions propounded by the church. In fact Thomism was describing the faith, not of the great religious geniuses, but of the simple medieval laymen whose religion was essentially obedience to the church.

Another and more characteristically modern account of faith presents it as a kind of betting. It is said that we cannot know whether there is a God but we may decide to bet our lives that there is. We may elect to act on the God-hypothesis, preferring to run the risk of believing that there is a God when in fact there is not, to that of believing that there is no God when in fact there is. This was the understanding of faith offered by Pascal in the famous Wager passage in his *Pensées*,[4] and by William James in his influential essay 'The Will to Believe'. But this again is remote from the state of mind of such men as the great prophets. They did not think of themselves as making a wager. They would never have granted the premiss that we cannot know whether God is real and therefore have to treat the question as a gamble. For they were convinced that they were conscious of God as acting towards them in the events of their own lives and of the history that was taking place around them. The Wager view of faith describes the condition, not of great primary religious figures, but of many people who have no personal sense of a divine presence but who are nevertheless impressed by the testimony of those who have.

Now without wanting to criticize one who commits himself to believe whatever a church teaches, or one who decides to bet his life on the God-hypothesis, I must insist that these are not faith in its most authentic forms; and that if we want to form a correct account of faith we must look at its classic exemplars. So then what is taking place when someone is in the state of mind which he describes as being vividly conscious of the presence and activity of God?

I believe that the very influential twentieth-century philosopher Ludwig Wittgenstein offers a useful hint when in his *Philosophical Investigations*[5] he draws attention to the significance of something that at first may seem quite trivial, namely puzzle pictures. There is, for example, the page covered apparently with random lines and dots which you may suddenly come to see as the picture of a human face; or the ambiguous duck-rabbit shape which you can see either as a duck's head facing left or as a rabbit's head facing right. In such cases two people or the same person at different times may perceive the same marks on paper in significantly different ways. Wittgenstein spoke of 'seeing as'; you see it as your mind interprets it, *as* a duck or *as* a rabbit. Now expand this notion into that of 'experiencing as' not only visually but through all the organs of perception functioning together. We experience situations in different ways as having different kinds of significance and so as rendering appropriate different practical responses. To come straight to the religious case, the prophets experienced their historical situation as one in which they were living under the sovereign claim of God and in which the appropriate way for them to act was as God's agents; whereas to most of their contemporaries the situation did not have this religious significance. When you look at the prophets' interpretation of Hebrew history embodied in the Old Testament you see that they were 'experiencing as' in a characteristic and consistent way. Where a secular historian would see at work various economic, social and geographical factors bringing about the rise and fall of cities and empires, the prophets saw behind all this the hand of God raising up and casting down and gradually fulfilling a purpose. When, for example, the Babylonians were at the gates of Jerusalem the prophet Jeremiah experienced this, not simply as a foreign political threat but also as God's judgment upon Israel for her national selfishness and irreligion. It is important to appreciate that this was not an interpretation in the sense of a theory imposed retrospectively upon remembered events. It was the way in which the prophet actually experienced and participated in these events at the time. He consciously lived in the situation interpreted in this way. He was 'experiencing as'.

Now 'experiencing as', like 'seeing as', is to an important extent voluntary, optional, uncompelled. You can see the figure on the paper either as a duck or as a rabbit, and in this case you can switch at will from one to the other. In the much more momentous and complex case of the experience of living our human life the change from one mode of 'experiencing as' to another has the quality of conversion. To most people most of the time life has a purely natural significance in which we are intelligent animals destined eventually to perish totally. But there may be a dawning of a new perspective in which our life comes to have religious significance as a gift from God, so that in all of life we are having to do with him, and he with us. Yet our human existence itself, considered apart from the interpretative responses of the human mind, remains ambigious and equally capable of being 'experienced as' in a religious or in a naturalistic manner.

I think it is perhaps worth noting that there is also an element of free response in two other main departments of human knowledge. One of these is sense perception. We normally experience our sensory impressions in terms of a three-dimensional world of objects in space around us. But that there is, at least in principle, something optional about this is shown by the fact that if someone believed that only his own consciousness existed and that the whole course of his experience was analogous to a dream, you could not dislodge him from this 'solipsism' (as it is called) by any logical argument. This does not indicate that our normal interpretation of our sense experience is doubtful, but that despite its indubitable character it is nevertheless an interpretation of data which are capable of being interpreted differently. Again, there is something optional about the awareness of moral obligation. Suppose some standard type of situation calling for a moral response – say, the sight of a bully cruelly hurting and injuring a helpless child. If someone were completely unmoved by such a situation, feeling no sympathy for the victim, no condemnation for the bully, and no sense of obligation to intervene, you could not prove to him by any logical argument that he is being blind to a moral reality. He would be a kind of moral solipsist.

I am suggesting then that faith is to be equated with the interpretative element within our experience – in sense perception; in moral responses; and in religion, where it is the interpretative activity by which we experience life as divinely created and ourselves as living in the unseen presence of God. This could, I hope, be a description of faith acceptable to both the believer and the sceptic. The sceptic, emphasizing the differences between religious experience and sense experience, will then say that faith, as a voluntary and gratuitous interpretation of life, is on a par with groundless superstitions and belief in fairies and witches. The believer on the other hand will go on to say that it is precisely through this ambiguity that God has chosen to reveal himself to us.

Let us explore this possibility of disclosure through the world's ambiguity a little further. We must ask: why should God want to present himself to his human creatures in such an indirect and uncertain way instead of revealing himself in some quite unambiguous fashion that would permit no possible room for doubt as to his reality? Perhaps the answer is that God is leaving men free in relation to himself. Perhaps he has deliberately created an ambiguous world for us just in order that we shall *not* be compelled to be conscious of him. But why not? Why should not the awareness of God, if he is there, be made as inescapable to us as the awareness of other human beings and of the world itself? In response to this question let us consider some of the differences that there must be between knowing God and knowing our neighbours. To know another human being is to know someone on the same level as ourselves. His existence does not necessarily or automatically make any difference to us; it may be a matter of indifference. The exception is when our awareness of another involves either love or hatred for that other. Then there is an analogy to the knowledge of God. God, if he is known to exist, can only be known as the One who makes a total difference for us. For he is known as infinitely higher than we, in worth as well as in power, and as having so made us that our own final self-fulfilment and happiness are also the fulfilment of his purpose for us. I cannot know that such a Being exists and be at the same time indifferent to him. For in knowing him I know myself as created and dependent, a creature on the periphery of existence, whose highest good lies in relation to the divine centre of reality. And so if the man who comes to be conscious of God in this way is to remain a free and responsible personality, the knowledge of God must not be forced upon him, but on the contrary, it must depend upon his own willingness to live in the presence of a higher being whose very existence, when we are conscious of it, sets us under an absolute claim.

Accordingly we can only come to know God by a free response to the ambiguous indications of his existence, a willingness to know him which then crystallizes into the experience of being in his presence. And the interpretative element within it, which I am identifying with religious faith, serves to safeguard our own separate personal existence over against the infinite being of God.[6]

I have mentioned Pascal's Wager. He also says, when speaking of this deliberate hiddenness of God for our sakes:

> It was not right that he should appear in a manner manifestly divine, and completely capable of convincing all men; but it was also not right that he should come in a manner so hidden that he could not be recognized by those who sincerely seek him. He has willed to make himself perfectly recognizable by those; and thus, willing to appear openly to those who seek him with all their heart, and hidden from those who flee from him with all their heart, he so arranges the knowledge of himself that he has given signs of himself, visible to those who seek him, and not to those who do not seek him. There is enough light for those who only desire to see, and enough obscurity for those who have a contrary disposition.[7]

3 *Is it then reasonable to believe in God?*

Is it then reasonable to believe in God? In the light of what

48

has been said in the preceding section the answer has to be: it is reasonable for some people, or for some people at some times, and not for other people at other times. Let me explain further.

First I must briefly make two philosophical points – fortunately points with which few philosophers in the present day would disagree. The first has to do with believing matters of fact – that is, with holding beliefs concerning what there is and what is the case. More particularly it has to do with reasonable or rational believing. By this I mean coming to believe on adequate grounds. As to what constitutes adequate grounds there can be no 'across the board' answer; criteria have to be established separately for each different subject-matter. And the point I want to make is this: the business of seeking knowledge is in practice simply the business of trying to come to reasonable or rational or adequately based beliefs. When we claim to know some matter of fact we are simply claiming to have adequate grounds for believing that same thing. For we have no other way of trying to determine its truth or falsity than by considering what grounds there are for believing it. And when we have come to a conclusion the claim that we make is necessarily in practice a claim about what it is reasonable or rational to believe. We are never in a position to make assertions about what the case is independently of assertions about what it is reasonable to believe to be the case.

The second point is a logical one and also, in my opinion, a matter of common sense, namely, that what it is or is not reasonable for a person to believe depends upon what data he has to go on. For example, it would have been unreasonable in the reign of Elizabeth I for anyone to believe that four hundred years later a man would be able to sit in a studio and his voice be heard and his image seen in homes all over the country. It would have been unreasonable because there were at that time no data available on the basis of which one might rationally have foreseen the development of radio and television. Or again, to take another type of case, if you know someone extremely well and know, for example, that it would have been morally and psychologically impossible for him to have committed a cold-blooded murder, it may be reasonable for you to believe that the accused is innocent even though the circumstantial evidence taken by itself would make it reasonable to believe him guilty. And in general, given an appropriate set of data – a relevant body of experience or information – it may be reasonable to believe something which it would not otherwise be reasonable to believe.

So – to link these points with our question – it is in principle quite possible for one person to have participated in experiences on the basis of which it is reasonable for him to believe in God and even unreasonable not to, while another person who has not participated in those experiences may equally reasonably not believe in God. And this is in fact, in my opinion, the situation. At least this is the situation in its simplest form though, as we shall see presently, the distinction between the two people is not usually nearly so clear-cut.

But let us look first at a clear-cut case – someone for whom belief in God is wholly reasonable because his experience gives him every right to be sure that God is real. As I suggested in the preceding section, the people to whom we must look are the prophets, saints, mystics, apostles and others who have been as overwhelmingly conscious of existing in the presence of God as of living in the material world. The consciousness of God in some of the great prophets of the Old Testament or in Jesus himself in the New Testament, as this is expressed through the biblical memories of them, was the awareness of an unseen personal presence and holy will and purpose which confronted them as truly and undeniably as did their neighbours or the environing physical world. But let us look particularly at Jesus' consciousness of God; for if we ourselves believe largely at second hand, on the strength of someone else's more direct and powerful religious experience, that someone else is for most of us Jesus of Nazareth.

Jesus' whole life was dominated by his consciousness of his heavenly Father. Even as a young boy, according to one of the traditions about him which Luke has preserved, he once lingered in the temple at Jerusalem after the Galilee caravan had departed, to listen to the rabbis and question them; and when his parents returned for him he said, 'Did

you not know that I was bound to be in my Father's house?'
(Luke 2.49, NEB). Between that time and the age of about
thirty, when Jesus came forward publicly as a teacher and
healer, we know nothing of his life, except that he was presumably living in Nazareth. Jesus' public career then began
with his baptism in the river Jordan by John the Baptist. At
this time Jesus had an experience of being recognized and
called as a son by his heavenly Father. During the following
two or three years he spent his days teaching and healing and
influencing a group of disciples. His teaching was wholly
about God, seeking to make the heavenly Father so real to
his hearers that they should begin to live consciously in
God's presence. Even Jesus' teaching about how men should
behave towards one another was at the same time teaching
about God. For right action is the action that comes naturally when one is consciously living in the presence of the
heavenly Father, so that to describe that style of life is also to
indicate something of the nature of God himself (see pp.
61–66). Again, all his healings were carried out in the name
of God and were seen by Jesus himself as manifestations of
God's power; the rule or kingdom of God which would one
day come universally was already manifesting itself in these
events. He taught his disciples to live in faith in God and in
conscious dependence upon him. During the brief climactic
period that bulks most largely in the recorded memory of the
early church – namely, Jesus' entry into Jerusalem followed
by his arrest, hurried trial during the night, and execution by
crucifixion – he was conscious all the time that he was walking with his destiny as God's representative, enacting his
heavenly Father's love even in the face of man's most violent
rejection. 'For even the Son of Man', he taught his disciples,
'did not come to be served but to serve, and to surrender his
life as a ransom for many' (Mark 10.45, NEB). And when the
soldiers were carrying out their grisly task he prayed, 'Father,
forgive them; they do not know what they are doing' (Luke
23.34, NEB). Even that mysterious cry from the cross, 'My
God, my God, why hast thou forsaken me?' (Mark 15.34,
NEB), whatever its significance may be,[8] shows that in this
extremity Jesus' mind was directed towards God; as it still
was when at the end 'Jesus gave a loud cry and said, "Father,

into thy hands I commit my spirit"; and with these words he died' (Luke 23.46, NEB).

In short then Jesus' whole life was coloured and dominated by his consciousness of God. God was as real to him as the sick whom he healed or the proud whom he condemned or the spiritually hungry whom he called to enter into a new life as God's children.

Now the question that has to be raised, in the light of the requirements of rational belief, is this: given the coherent lifelong experience which he consistently expressed as an experience of the presence and activity of God, was it reasonable for Jesus to believe in the reality of God? Notice that I am not asking: is it rational for someone else, who does not in any way share that experience, to believe in God on the basis of Jesus' (or anyone else's) reports? I am asking the quite different question whether it is reasonable for the religious man himself (and I am thinking of the strongest instance known to us, namely Jesus of Nazareth) to believe in God on the basis of his own compelling religious experience? For his situation was that he could not help believing in God. I think it is clear that to reject his awareness of the divine Thou would have been to deny his own sanity as a cognizing being, as one whose consciousness is reliably affected by external reality. This would be as fundamentally absurd as rejecting one's perception of the surrounding physical world and of other people; it would amount to an act of intellectual suicide.

And yet to see this is not to settle the question. The fact that someone cannot help believing something because his experience compels him to believe it, does not prove that what he believes is true. There can be compelling delusions as well as compelling perceptions. There are people in mental hospitals whose distinctive experience is such that it is reasonable for them to believe that they are Napoleon or that the world is made of cheese or that demons speak to them threateningly out of the air. And although we recognize that their beliefs and reasonings may follow logically enough from their private obsessive delusions or hallucinations, we nevertheless regard them as insane. And this is also the blunt question that we have to ask ourselves concerning Jesus of

Nazareth and the other religious figures who report their experience of the presence of God. The question is not so much one of reasons and reasoning: it is the more fundamental question of reason or sanity. The issue is not so much the rationality of the belief as the rationality of the believer. Do we account him sane or insane? If insane, we dismiss his distinctive beliefs along with himself. If sane, we acknowledge his right as a rational person to believe what his own religious experience compels him to believe.

How then do we decide whether Jesus was, in the governing principle of his life, insane, and his whole activity and influence therefore based upon delusion, or whether in fact he was more truly in contact with reality than the rest of us, so that his teaching is a crucial pointer for us to the character of reality? There can be no proof either way independently of what it is reasonable for anyone, given their own personal experience, to believe. The question is in practice decided by our own individual response to the person of Jesus. In the end if we face the issue fully we either find ourselves seeing in him the ultimate of human sanity and therefore as being for us, in New Testament language, 'the way, the truth and the life', or else as embodying the ultimate of human delusion, an attractive lunatic who would mislead us into the folly of a life built upon illusion. Our choice, when we dare to make it, is a choice with our whole nature between two utterly incompatible conceptions of human sanity, two utterly opposed readings of our human situation, the one or other of which is forced upon us as we confront seriously the claims and call of Jesus of Nazareth.

There is, however, a wider background situation within which this choice has to be made and which can itself influence our choice. This is our understanding of the universe as a whole, in so far as it is known to us, our understanding of it such that we find it *possible* or *impossible* that it all exists by the will and within the purpose of a transcendent Creator. This question is the sphere of natural theology, which used to have the aim of proving that God exists but which today has the more modest aim of showing it to be *possible* that God exists. The contribution of natural theology to religious faith is to show the possibility of God; but it cannot do more than this. What used to be regarded as demonstrations of the existence of God are really arguments for the real possibility of divine existence.

For when we try to think about this infinitely fascinating universe in which we live we find that we are faced in the end with sheer mystery – the mystery of existence, of why there is a universe at all. And this mystery is not dissipated by the marvellous expansion of our scientific knowledge of the intricate interrelations of things and thus of how the universe functions and according to what regularities. For no increment of understanding of this kind can tell us *why* there is matter in the first place and what purpose, if any, ordered matter serves. This ultimate mystery confronting us at the final boundaries of thought does not prove that there *is* a divine Creator – a first cause, or prime mover, or necessary being, or cosmic designer – but it does present this to us as a real possibility. In our deepest reflections, when our thoughts are not confined within the borders of some special discipline – chemistry, physics, astronomy, or whatever it may be – but when simply as human beings we are facing our total environment in its totality, we find that we cannot rule out the possibility of God. The ultimate mystery of existence and order, intelligence and value, leaves us with a question which cannot be erased, a question to which the answer may be – God.

It is within this wider background-situation in which as thinking beings we can see the possibility of God that religious experience may properly convince a person that God is indeed real. And it is within this same situation that we face the person of Jesus of Nazareth, and the crucial question of sanity or delusion with which his life and teaching confronts us.

Let us then consider the case of someone who is in some real degree drawn to affirm the sanity of Jesus and therefore of all that he stands for; or at least who is unable to dismiss him as profoundly disoriented to reality and his teachings as delusions. This is, after all, the actual position of many of us. Is it reasonable for us to believe in God? Is it reasonable to believe in God, and to try to live on the basis that God is real, because we believe in the total sanity of Jesus of

Nazareth and therefore believe that the dominating experience of his life, the experience of living in the presence of God, was not delusory?

Surely we must say that just as one, such as Jesus himself, who is overwhelmingly conscious of God, has the right to claim to be believing in God on adequate grounds, so others on their own lower levels of religious experience, centring upon their response to Jesus, can also claim to be believing reasonably. Such a claim is rational to the extent to which as rational individuals we are in fact drawn by the reality before us, which is the person of Jesus of Nazareth. We shall only be so drawn if his claims find a sufficient echo in our own experience – if his total openness to others in their human needs, and his way of life based upon self-giving love, lay a strong enough claim upon our own lives, and if his teaching about the heavenly Father becomes credible to us and more than credible in the light of Jesus' life. If our own experience as a whole leads us to respond on his own terms to Jesus of Nazareth this response will then be as rational as we ourselves are. The moral is: if you trust in your own rationality then act upon what you cannot help believing.[9]

4 *What has the Bible to contribute?*

Building upon the last two sections it is now possible to describe the function of the Bible within the continuing process of God's self-disclosure and man's response. For what I have said about religious faith reflects a revolution that has taken place in Christian thinking both about the nature of revelation and about the part played within it by the Bible.

The older view was that revelation consists in God imparting to men various religious truths which would otherwise have remained unknown to them. These truths – such as that God is three in one and one in three – were supposed to have been revealed either by being taught by an infallible church (the Roman Catholic view) or by being contained in an infallible book (the Protestant view). In contrast the newer view abandons infallibility-claims for both the church and Bible. Instead it sees both of these as aspects of the fallible human response to God's self-revealing activity. God has revealed his presence and his nature by acting in relation to mankind, and men have received the revelation when by faith they have experienced the events in question *as* mediating God's presence and activity. I have already suggested that this response is religious faith in the basic and primary sense of that term (see pp. 45–48). We noted certain great moments in biblical history in which prophets or apostles saw God at work. Apart from that response of faith, the events in question were ambiguous, capable of being experienced either religiously or non-religiously; but in conjunction with a human faith-response they took on a revelatory character. To the eyes of faith, history had become transparent to the divine presence.

On this view God has not revealed religious truths or theological propositions to us but has instead revealed his own nature by expressing it in his actions in relation to mankind. He has revealed his presence and his character in basically the same way that a human being does – by acting so that others feel the impact of his presence and become conscious of the attitudes, values and purposes embodied in his actions. And if we ask why God has revealed himself in this indirect way which depends for its success upon an answering human response of faith, instead of making himself unmistakably evident to all by some overwhelming display of omnipotence, the answer must be that he is concerned to preserve our finite human freedom in relation to himself. He has not merely given us the freedom to obey or disobey him once we are aware of him, but the more fundamental freedom to be or fail to be conscious of him in the first place. This is our 'cognitive freedom' over against God, preserved by the 'epistemic distance' at which he has set us by our emergence within the evolutionary process as intelligent and responsible animals who had yet to become conscious of their maker.

What does all this imply concerning the Bible? The important fact about the books of the Bible is that they were written from within the particular strand of history through which Christianity believes that God has most powerfully made his presence felt, the strand which culminates in the coming of the Christ. They record that history as it was experienced by men of faith who were aware of God at work within it. The Old Testament contains the sacred writings of Jews over a period of nearly a thousand years, reflecting their consciousness of God's activity in delivering them from slavery in Egypt and settling them in Palestine as a people in a special relationship with himself, a chosen instrument for the salvation of the world; and recording also their fallings away from this vocation and God's drastic recalling of them by means of calamitous events in their history such as the national exile in Babylon. This was the significance of these events as they were interpreted by the great prophets. Through the prophets' words, as remembered and recorded, God is increasingly revealed in the Old Testament as maker and lord of the whole world and not only of the Jews themselves, and as a careful shepherd and loving father as well as a just and all-powerful judge.

One could describe at length this unfolding Old Testament revelation of God, but I shall instead pass on to the New Testament. For the Christian understanding of the Old Testament is that it records the long preparation for the coming of Christ. But it is the New Testament itself that reflects the high point of God's self-revelation in the life of Jesus of Nazareth; and accordingly it is appropriate to discuss the questions of biblical inspiration and authority and historical reliability in terms of the New Testament documents.

The New Testament is a dossier of documents of various kinds which were produced within what has been called the Christ-event – the whole complex of occurrences consisting of the life of Jesus and the beginnings of the church. This dossier includes three memoirs of Jesus (the gospels of Mark, Matthew and Luke) produced by now unknown Christians between one and two generations after Jesus' death and embodying the memories and traditions concerning him that were circulating within the church at that time; another memoir (John's gospel), probably written about a generation later, which interweaves symbolic stories with historical memories in order to show the meaning of Jesus' life and death and resurrection; a history of the early church (Acts), including a portion of the travel-diary of a member of Paul's party on one of his journeys (Acts 16.10–17 and 20.5 onwards); letters by church leaders to the Christian communities in various places; bits of early sermons embedded in Acts; and a strange visionary pamphlet (the Revelation of St John). These are presumably not the only writings produced within and reflecting the character of the Christ-event, but they are the only ones which have been preserved for later ages. When the early church collected together what we now call the New Testament it was trying to assemble all the Christian documents it could that had come down from the apostolic age. The criterion employed was apostolic or near-apostolic authorship; and the names of specific apostles – Matthew, John, James, Peter – and of the near-apostolic figures of Paul, Mark, Luke and Jude became attached to writings which were believed to have been used within the church since the age of the apostles. We know now that many of these specific attributions are either mistaken or at least doubtful. Thus judged by their traditional titles the documents are false. But this is merely to say that their titles are false. The documents themselves are authentic Christian writings from the apostolic church – the church at the time when some of the apostles were still alive and when there were many in the churches who had known them and heard their preaching about Jesus. As such the New Testament is our point of nearest contact with Jesus of Nazareth. He is reflected there in the writings of a community in which memories of him, flowing into a kind of corporate memory, lived powerfully on. These memories became part of the consciousness of the church, interacting in its life with the other factors that affected it and becoming embodied in documentary form as the New Testament picture of Jesus as Lord and Saviour.

The precise historical accuracy of the New Testament documents is at this distance of time very difficult, indeed impossible, to determine. The gospels are certainly not to be treated as though they were direct eye-witness reports of Jesus' doings and utterances; for the first of them to be written, Mark, was probably compiled about thirty years after Jesus' death. Early tradition says that Mark's gospel was based on the preaching of St Peter, and there may be some element of recollection derived from Peter within it. But generally the sayings and stories which compose the gospels are literary pebbles shaped and polished by many different hands and eventually fitted by the church into the mosaic picture that we now have of Jesus as the Christ. As the sayings and stories were carried from one audience to another, and were no doubt heightened in preaching and sharpened for use in debate, they gradually developed to the form in which they were set down in our gospels. We cannot now be sure that any of the sayings are precise verbatim reports of Jesus' own words, or that any of the narratives are in detail accurate descriptions of what happened. What we are seeing and hearing is Jesus imprinted in the memories and interests and understanding of his followers and of others who followed them, all organized in the light of the church's faith-response to Jesus as the risen Lord and Saviour.

And yet through all this complexity of transmission there does come through the documents an unforgettably challenging moral teaching, and the coherent impression of a profoundly serene and disturbing personality in whom are focused upon us claims and challenges and promises that are ultimate. This Christ is undoubtedly real, for he affects us and our lives today. And the New Testament writings fulfil their function as a medium through which he encounters us.

What then should be meant by the 'inspiration' of the Bible? That which distinguishes it from secular, non-inspired histories of the same events is the fact that the Bible expresses the religious faith of its writers. It is not neutral chronicling but history interpreted by faith – the faith by which the prophets saw God at work in Hebrew history and by which the apostles found him present among them in the life of Jesus of Nazareth. And the faith of the writers is their inspiration; to say that they were inspired is simply to say that they were people to whom God had succeeded in revealing himself. Their writings are inspired because they express the faith-response in which God's activity became revelatory to the writers. And when later readers – such as ourselves today – respond to the Bible by sharing the faith of its writers it thereby becomes revelatory to us also. Thus the Bible is itself a channel of revelation. produced by faith and evoking faith.

NOTES

1. Fred Hoyle, *The Black Cloud*, Harmondsworth and Baltimore: Penguin, 1960, p. 203.

2. C. D. Broad, *The Mind and Its Place in Nature*, London: Kegan Paul, and New York: Harcourt, 1925, chs. 12 and 14; A. C. Ewing,*The Fundamental Questions of Philosophy*, London: Routledge, and New York: Macmillan, 1952, chs. 5, 6 and 11; Paul Badham, *Christian Beliefs about Life after Death*, London: Macmillan, and New York: Barnes & Noble, 1976, chs. 6–8; H. D. Lewis, *The Elusive Mind*, London: Allen & Unwin, and New York: Humanities Press, 1969.

3. Bertrand Russell, *The Impact of Science on Society*, New York: Columbia University Press, 1951, and London: Allen & Unwin, 1952, p. 114.

4. Blaise Pascal, *Pensées*, ed. Brunschvicg, No. 233 (London: J. M. Dent & Sons, and New York: E. P. Dutton, 1932, pp. 66f.).

5. Ludwig Wittgenstein, *Philosophical Investigations*, Oxford: Basil Blackwell, and New York: Macmillan, 1953, Part II.xi.

6. I have written about the nature of faith more fully along these lines in *Faith and Knowledge*, 2nd ed., London: Fontana paperback, and Cleveland, Ohio: Fountain paperback, 1974.

7. Pascal's *Pensées*, No. 430 (p. 118).

8. See D. E. Nineham, *The Gospel of Saint Mark*, Harmondsworth and Baltimore: Penguin, 1963, pp. 427–9.

9. For a fuller development of this position, see my *Arguments for the Existence of God*, London: Macmillan, 1970, and New York: Herder & Herder, 1971, pp. 107–16.

III   Christian Faith in the World Today

1 *What practical difference does faith make?*

When we consider what it is to believe anything, we see that to believe genuinely in the reality of God cannot fail to make a very large difference, both at particular moments and pervasively throughout our life as a whole. Modern philosophical discussions have found an important clue to the nature of belief in that great majority of our beliefs which we are not at the moment holding in consciousness. For as well as that (if anything) which we are consciously believing at the moment we have an enormous number of stored beliefs which are waiting to come into consciousness and/or to affect our actions when they are relevant to what is taking place. For example, we all learned as children that the battle of Hastings was fought in 1066 or that George Washington became President in 1789 but we have certainly not been continuously and explicitly thinking of these facts ever since. We can correctly be said to have believed them since our youth, and yet most of the time this has been true of us without our actually thinking of them at all. What form then have these stored beliefs taken? They have existed as *dispositions to act on the basis that* – to act on the basis, for example, that the battle of Hastings was fought in 1066. In this case such a disposition might lead one to say '1066' when asked for the date of that battle; to agree when someone mentioned this as its date and to disagree or correct him if he offered a different date; to draw inferences from our information (inferring, for instance, that 1966 was the nine hundredth anniversary of the event); and so on. Or again, to believe that today is Thursday involves being all day in the complex state of readiness appropriate to its being Thursday – expecting this rather than that to happen, being prepared to do this and not that. One might conceivably hold a belief dispositionally for years or even for the rest of one's life without its being activated; or on the other hand one might find oneself frequently or for continuous periods in situations to which that belief is relevant.

All our beliefs have a dispositional aspect. (There are also other aspects of belief with which we are not directly concerned at the moment – principally the having or having had the proposition before one's mind, together with an assenting attitude to it.) To believe any proposition, let us call it *p*, involves either currently acting on the basis of *p* or else being in a dispositional state to act on that basis if and when *p* is practically relevant. The connection between believing *p* and acting or being effectively disposed to act on the basis of it is such that it is not possible to believe *p* and act (except in charade and deception) on the basis of not-*p*. In other words our deliberate actions are an infallible indication of our beliefs. The propostion that we believe is, by definition, the one on which we act.

I think this is something well known to common sense. Suppose someone professes to be magically immune to fire so that he can walk unharmed through flames and pick up hot coals. If he does confidently pick up burning coals or walk without hesitation into a blazing fire we should say that he really does believe that fire cannot hurt him. But if he shrinks back from the flames like anyone else, we know then that he really believes that fire will hurt him. The test of his belief is found in his actions. A real belief inevitably makes its appropriate difference to the way we behave.

What then does it mean to believe in the reality of God as the heavenly Father whose nature was taught and shown by Jesus? According to this account of belief it involves being in a dispositional state to act on the basis that God, so conceived, is real; and the extent to which a person *really* believes in God is precisely the extent to which he or she lives on that basis.

The question: 'What is God like?' and 'How does one act on the basis that such a God is real?' are two aspects of a single question. From the fact that God's nature is of a certain kind it follows that a certain pattern of human behaviour is appropriate. And conversely to say that a certain pattern of behaviour is appropriate within the divine ordering of the universe is to indicate what God's nature is. And so a distinctive pattern of behaviour is rendered appropriate by belief in the reality of God as he was revealed in Jesus; and this pattern constitutes the Christian ethic. This ethic is a general description of the way in which anyone, who genuinely believes in God as Jesus revealed him, behaves. Accordingly, to present the claims of the Christian way of life is also and thereby to proclaim the reality and nature of God.

This means that the Christian ethic is not, as has often been assumed, a set of divine commands or divinely authorized rules. It also means that the vexed question of the special motive for the Christian life does not arise. If we think of the Christian ethic as a body of commandments, most of which generally run counter to our natural human interests and desires, then clearly some extraordinary counter-balancing inducement is necessary in the form of either promised rewards or threatened punishments. So heaven and hell are mobilized as sanctions for the Christian life.

But the view which I am suggesting on the basis of the dispositional analysis of belief is widely different from this and comes, I believe, much closer to the moral teaching of Jesus. Such collections of his sayings as the Sermon on the Mount provide a description, with illustrations drawn from the daily life of Galilee in the first century AD, of the way in which anyone who genuinely and wholeheartedly believes in the heavenly Father will naturally tend to live.

We can perhaps see this most clearly by contrast. If we believe that we are, as the non-religious vision sees us, only intelligent animals enjoying or suffering a brief existence and destined to perish utterly like the other animals, then a moral policy of self-preservation and self-aggrandisement over against the rival egoisms of others constitutes a rational response to our human situation. But if on the contrary we believe – as an operative belief which is built into our dispositional state – that this is God's world and that we are in his hands, we shall lack or tend to lose the basic anxiety about our existence which inevitably produces egoism; nor

63

shall we be concerned constantly to safeguard our own interests against the rest of the world. For if God has created us ultimately for joyous fellowship with himself, then our fundamental interests and our place within his universe are secure. Again, if other human beings are not inevitable rivals in a struggle for existence but fellow children of our heavenly Father, then the call to love our neighbour as ourself simply spells out the meaning of God's reality for us. To love one's neighbour as oneself is to see self and neighbour as objects of the same divine love, and as called to mutual service each as God's agent in relation to the other.

This vision of the world and of human existence in its relation to God was often expressed by Jesus in an imperative form – for example. 'But what I tell you is this: Love your enemies and pray for your persecutors; only so can you be children of your heavenly Father, who makes his sun rise on good and bad alike, and sends the rain on the honest and the dishonest' (Matt. 5.44, NEB). I think that Jesus put it as a command because he was both presenting a conception of God in terms of its practical implications, and presenting a way of life in terms of the conviction about God which makes it reasonable. The imperative form is due to the fact that Jesus was not merely describing God and his relation to the world in an academically detached fashion but was challenging his hearers with the concrete claim of the truth upon their own lives. For when we are first confronted with his vision and its very practical and immediate personal implications, it presents us with a profoundly challenging call – a call to enter into a new vision of the universe and a new way of life which stand in strong contrast to our prevailing non-religious assumptions and practices. Hence we find the dual note in Jesus' teaching – on the one hand the naturalness of his style of living for one who sees himself as existing in the unseen presence of God, and yet on the other hand the daunting summons to turn one's whole self round to see the world in this way.

But is not the other-regarding outlook, the attitude of love for the neighbour, contrary to our basically selfish human nature and therefore unable to be achieved merely by a new vision of the world? On the contrary: it seems that human nature is capable of developing either into self-regarding egoism or into openness to others, depending upon the individual's most important experiences and operative beliefs. This is shown by findings in child psychology. The child who believes and feels himself to be the object of a dependable love on the part of the effective higher powers in his universe, namely his parents, tends to develop an open and loving attitude not only to his parents but to people in general. On the other hand the child who feels deprived of love and is uncertain of surrounding affection feels basically insecure and tends to develop the opposite pattern of 'affectionless' reactions, becoming enclosed, suspicious and defensively egoistic. The awareness of being loved brings out the best in our nature, opening doors within us to a positive and zestful participation in human life and to a charitable, outward-going attitude to others. It does not do this by setting up any special motive or inducement but simply because human nature is made this way. Openness to others is a natural response to the fundamental security of being loved by the operative power of our universe.[1]

The principle disclosed in child psychology applies also to adults. In so far as his nature is not too deeply warped by bad early experiences, the adult who believes in the cosmic love we call God tends to manifest what St Paul called the harvest of the Spirit, which he said is 'love, joy, peace, patience, kindness, goodness, fidelity, gentleness, and self-control' (Gal. 5.22, NEB).

The situation then is this: we all prevailingly live in the world as in our heart of hearts we really believe it to be. For the fundamental (if usually unformulated) aim of any sane person is to live in terms of reality and to pursue in the real world the good which our nature sets for us, which we call happiness. Hence the different moral policies and patterns of behaviour which people adopt reflect, not different basic aims in life but different conceptions of the world in which they are living, its determining powers and laws. Jesus' style of life differed from the ordinary ways of the world because his operative conception of the universe differed from that of others; and to come to share his vision of reality is also to be drawn towards his way of life.[2]

This does not, however, mean that the Christian life today is an imitation of the life of Jesus of Nazareth in first-century Palestine. All that one can say in general is that it is a sharing of Jesus' vision of the world in its relation to God and then a living in terms of that vision in one's own very different time and place and circumstances. What this requires concretely has to be discovered by responsible engagement in the various situations which constitute our life. Discerning what love demands in the large and small decisions that confront us is the creative aspect of our existence as persons living in relation with other persons in God's universe. There is a universally valid moral principle – to value and respect others as you value and respect yourself. But there can be no universally valid moral rules to spell out the consequences of this in practice, because the structures of human situations vary so widely in different cultural circumstances. Accordingly we have to use our individual and corporate judgment. But of course this does not mean that we have continually to start from the beginning as though every fresh situation were quite unprecedented. In its full concreteness every situation is unique just as every leaf and blade of grass is unique; but there are nevertheless obvious similarities and recurrences in human affairs so that decisions made in the past are relevant to the making of decisions now. There is in fact a great body of accumulated and tested experience, wisdom and precedent to help us, although this can never remove from us our own final responsibility for our actions.

Christian decision-making in personal, social and political life is one of the immensely important subjects which unfortunately cannot be pursued properly within the limited plan of this short book.

2 *Being a member of the church*

The church (meaning by it all the Christian bodies considered together) is in a quite precise sense a necessary evil – and to that extent a good. It is an evil because the corruption of the best is the worst, and the church is the human corruption of the kingdom of God which came on earth in the person of Jesus of Nazareth. It is because the church ought to be startlingly better that in being mediocre it is bad. But, good or bad, the church was inevitable; for Jesus' message is one that inevitably draws people together. It cannot be fully responded to in isolation, for part of the response consists in a changed attitude towards other people. Jesus did not appeal, as a philosopher might, for the purely intellectual response of individuals who were to remain separate and unrelated. He was creating a community, a living corporate entity, a body of people of which the original nucleus was the group of apostles. This Christian body has lived on from century to century, its composition gradually changing all the time like that of our own bodies and yet with a visible continuity through time.

However, this church which Jesus founded has today become a stumbling block to almost anyone who is drawn to him. For the life of the church falls far below the level of the life of God's reign on earth as we see this bursting forth in the early Christian community. The New Testament church as it is reflected in the book called the Acts of the Apostles was (to use its own language) filled with the Holy Spirit. It was pervaded by the spirit of Jesus of Nazareth, now exalted as Christ and Lord (the Holy Spirit and the spirit of Jesus are identified at several points in the New Testament). It is true that there were quarrels and rifts and deep differences of opinion; but the force which eventually overcame these differences and preserved the essential unity of the Christian community was the spirit of the risen Lord working among his disciples. However, within three or four centuries the church had become almost indistinguishably blended with the declining Roman Empire and the spirit that prevailed within it was that of imperial and, later, pontifical Rome. Human power-structures originally developed to preserve order in Europe during the slow collapse of the Empire now acquired their own momentum and have largely dominated the church ever since. The Reformation of the sixteenth century was a violent revolt against this domination. But within a century the Reformation had become a parallel rival establishment, changing many of the forms of the ecclesiastical power-structure but equally dominated by authoritarianism, attachment to property and unimaginative lovelessness towards the outsider.

What has happened since then is that the cultural, social and economic character of Western society has taken a new turn, leaving the church behind. This new turn is a vast and complex phenomenon which is studied from a Christian point of view in Harvey Cox's fascinating book *The Secular City*.[3] Its elements are the scientific and technological revolution of our time, including automation and cybernation; the secularization of society; the communications explosion; and the increasingly rapid social changes involved in the growth of immense conurbations of millions of people. All this is rapidly producing a secular society with a secular attitude to life within which the ideas of the supernatural and of God; providence, revelation, miracles; mystery and worship; eternal life and the kingdom of heaven, are seen as but the dreams and fairy tales of bygone ages.

Now from one point of view this must seem sad and depressing. For it means that the churches as they have existed in pre-secular society are doomed to die with the environment which formed and sustained them. The churches as they now are cannot survive for very long. Nor should we wish to prolong their life beyond the point at which new and more viable forms of Christian life have become apparent. Indeed what is to be feared is rather that the present churches, unadapted to the new age, *will* contrive to survive – but by going culturally underground and becoming totally irrelevant to the on-going life of mankind. In these days when the obsolescence of the church's modes of thought and life is so painfully evident, but while there is still no clear vision of the right ways in a changing world, it is increasingly difficult for Christians acutely aware of the need for new forms to continue within the old. There has accordingly been a dramatic drop in the number of candidates for the Christian priesthood and ministry and a continuous movement out of these vocations into forms of secular service. And the resulting danger is that as the more radical spirits leave it the church will thereby become more and more conservative and defensive so that instead of transforming itself it will persist as a spiritual ghetto, fundamentalist in thought and pietistically criticizing a world which it cannot understand.

If the church manages to reform itself to serve God in the new age, how will it do so? It is clear to nearly all of us that radical changes are urgently needed, and yet there is no concensus as to what these changes should be. In this situation it is open to every concerned individual to help to form Christian policies for the renewal of the church.

The church's problems are of course different in different lands. In Britain there are too many too small congregations (of whatever denomination), generally weak and dispirited, stoically 'carrying on' with little real impetus or joy. In the United States the problem is the opposite one of large and flourishing churches which are tempted to be so closely integrated with the American way of life that they lose their specifically Christian insights and standards of judgment. The problem in each case is not how to make the churches more successful (for success depends upon many factors, some of which are quite outside the churches' control) but how to make them more authentically Christian. The most fruitful thinking in this field is likely to be done by some of the clergy, who are closest to the problem and who are in a position to put their ideas experimentally into practice and to develop them within the concrete situations in which the church must act.

On the face of it, it would seem that the reunion of the still divided branches of Christianity must be an important key to the situation. However, many radical Christians today, and particularly the new generation which has not been involved in the struggles and hard-won advances of the ecumenical movement during the last quarter of a century, have come to look upon the churches as so nearly dead that the question of their reunion is unimportant. Why should we bother to unite corpses? But I should like to enter a plea for the continuing importance of church reunion today. It is important, not as a device for preserving the status quo by mergers and retrenchment, but in order to release the active core of the church (including of course the clergy) from the frustrating task of maintaining a self-defeating plethora of institutions. They would then be able to work together and reinforce one another instead of dissipating their energies in small parallel and even competing efforts. At the same time the general shake-up involved should open the way to all sorts of fruitful experiments in both the church's worship and its service to the world. A further important by-product of the effort towards Christian unity is that since the obstacles lie in the realm of our differing human traditions and habits we are compelled, in order to overcome them, to go behind these to the Christian starting-point of our response to Jesus of Nazareth.

Let me offer a purely personal glimpse, primarily with the British situation in mind, of what the church could be like in, say, ten years time. There should be about a third or a quarter as many churches and chapels as there are now, as a result of local unions made possible by denominational unions involving the Church of England, the Church of Scotland, and all the Free Churches. (Union with an internally reformed Roman Catholic Church must be hoped for at a later stage.) In most churches both a liturgical type of worship continuing that of the Anglican prayer book, and a relatively non-liturgical type of worship continuing that of most of the Free Churches, will take place at different times on Sundays, no doubt with progressive interaction between them as the two constituencies mingle and learn from one another. Organizationally the united church will, I hope, be roughly modelled on the Church of South India, with elected bishops who are both pastors to pastors and chairmen of governing committees. But most important of all, the united church will be able to assign appropriately trained representatives to study the various aspects of the society in which it lives and to lead experiments in Christian service to that society. The church will have energy and resources to look outwards and to serve God by serving the neighbour. We need not look or hope further than a situation in which the church is truly and recognizably the church, for what then happens to it and through it will be in line with God's purpose for it.

3 *Orthodoxy and unorthodoxy*

Within the churches we live today in a time of theological

turmoil. On the Protestant side, in 1963 John Robinson's *Honest to God* crystallized a widespread suspicion that our traditional ecclesiastical images of God are too small and are inadequate to the limitless divine Reality; and in 1977 *The Myth of God Incarnate*, by seven Anglican and Free Church theologians, brought to the surface a widespread sense that traditional incarnational and trinitarian language has got stuck in an uncritically literal usage, and needs to be re-understood. Both books evoked strong but contradictory reactions. From some quarters came condemnation and calls for the authors to resign their church orders. In other quarters there was a very positive interest and appreciation. On the Catholic side Hans Küng's *On Being a Christian* (1974, ET 1977) and Edward Schillebeeckx's *Jesus: An Experiment in Christology* (1974, ET 1979), together with their other books, have revealed a trend which moves independently in the same general direction as the new Protestant thinking. The Catholic works, too, have evoked strong but contradictory reactions – a very considerable public welcome, but also official warnings and reprimands from the Vatican. All these writings, both Protestant and Catholic, have been concerned with the Christian assimilation of new knowledge both from the sciences and from the historical study of the scriptures and of Christian origins. A further element, stirring Christian thought from another angle, is the rapidly growing and now well-established Western Christian awareness of the theological problem posed by the fact that Christianity is not the only world faith but one of several – a problem which I shall discuss directly in the next chapter.

In this situation, in which so many traditional concepts are being reconsidered, theological thinking undoubtedly involves certain dangers. There is the danger of a rethinking of Christianity which is so radical that the product is no longer Christian. And there is the danger of a failure to rethink which results in Christianity becoming a specialized interest of the few, wrapped in an outmoded world-view which is increasingly irrelevant to modern life.

These opposite dangers raised the question, How is Christianity to be defined? What is its essence? 'Profession of faith', i.e. the holding of certain beliefs? A life oriented in discipleship to Jesus? Baptism and membership of the church? One can argue for each of these, and other, answers. I would suggest, however, that the very idea of an essence of Christianity, and a search for that essence, is not the most appropriate approach to the issue of Christian identity. For in an important sense Christianity (or any other religion) does not have an unchanging essence; it is not a static entity but a living strand of history, continuously growing into the future. Christianity is the historical movement that was initiated by the impact of Jesus upon a group of first-century Jews. In all probability, Jesus himself did not know that he was launching a new religion; for he seems to have expected the end of the present age to come within a very short time. But nevertheless, without intending to, he did in fact become the founder of a new movement which has reached global proportions. And its 'essence', if one wants to use that term, lies in its origin. This origin in the life and teaching of Jesus, and all that follows from this, distinguishes the Christian strand of religious history from, say, the Muslim or the Buddhist strand. Christianity is the movement which looks back to Jesus as its originator and which has accordingly been centrally influenced by its communal memory of him, enshrined in its scriptures. And to the eyes of the historian, a Christian is one who is part of this distinctive strand of religious history.

What, then, is Christian belief? From the historical point of view Christian belief is what Christians believe. And this has always been various – widely various in the early centuries, much less so in mediaeval Christendom, and very various again in the modern world and perhaps never more so than today. Thus the question of how the lordship of Jesus (that is, his worthiness to attract disciples) is to be understood philosophically was the subject of a tremendous, many-sided debate in the early Christian centuries, which was only 'settled' when the Roman Emperor insisted upon a uniform belief-system for Christendom. But there have always been those who have been dissatisfied with the official formulae; and now that such dissenters are no longer burned at the stake, they are more numerous than ever. Again, the understanding of the meaning of Jesus' death has taken a wide variety of forms. In the early centuries the idea was common that on the cross Jesus had defeated the devil and thereby won back our human freedom.

But after Anselm's work in the eleventh century this imagery was largely superseded by the idea that Jesus' death had constituted a 'satisfaction' to God in atonement for the wrong of man's disobedience. At the Reformation the penal-substitutionary theory, according to which Jesus bore on our behalf the punishment justly due for human sin, and thereby enabled God to forgive us, became widespread within Protestantism. These are the official theories. And yet today there are many thoughtful Christians for whom none of them is at all attractive or plausible. Again, the nature and authority of the Bible has come to be very differently understood during the last century and a half, as a result of intensive historical study. Yet again, beliefs about judgment, heaven and hell have changed greatly over the modern period, and some of the ideas that were seriously entertained in the mediaeval period and later now seem merely grotesque. In short, instead of being a solid monolithic system Christian theology is a living organism which has evolved over the centuries, adapting itself to a changing cultural environment. And so we cannot rule out a development of Christian thought on the grounds that it differs from the state of Christian belief at some other time. Nor can we who are now part of this history legislate for future generations.

But on the other hand the Christian churches, as human organizations, are perfectly entitled to try to control and limit theological reflection among their own members. A voluntary society can set its own conditions for membership; and a society which takes the Thirty-nine Articles of the Church of England, or the Westminster Confession of the Presbyterian Churches, or some other of the great historic confessions of faith, as definitive is entitled to rule that only those who wholeheartedly subscribe to that confession may be members, or office-bearers, of that society. In fact, however, apart from rare spasms, the main Christian churches no longer in practice operate in that way today. They all embrace within themselves the full spectrum of theological opinion, from the most traditionally conservative to the most radically experimental.

Indeed within each of the main denominations today there are, in effect, two Christianities, or two understandings of Christianity, some members adhering to one, some to the other, and some perhaps fluctuating between them. According to one understanding, Christians believe in the verbal inspiration and absolute authority of the Bible, and in Adam and Eve, the virgin birth of Jesus, his unique status as God incarnate, his bodily resurrection, heaven and hell, and the need to evangelize the world because there is salvation only by taking Jesus as one's Lord and Saviour; and Christians give to charity but do not become heavily involved in efforts to change the political and economic structures of the world. According to the other understanding, Christians seek to be disciples of Jesus, whilst interpreting him theologically in a variety of ways, and seek to love God and love their neighbours, both individually and by working for liberation from economic, social and political repression. They see the Bible as a record of vital religious experience within a particular strand of human history; and accept that there are other strands with other experiences and other scriptures.

Conscious that the new contemporary form of Christian understanding differs from the traditional norms enshrined in the great confessions of the past, Christians of the second kind are often tempted to leave the institutional church and to live out their Christian discipleship independently of it. However, the more this happens the more the church will lag behind the ever-changing human consciousness and become ghettoes in which life is lived in terms of an antique mythology. Such extreme poliarization could only be disastrous. For each kind of Christianity in fact needs the other. There is a powerful stream of authentic religious devotion within the conservative-evangelical world which seems to require a simplistic conceptuality, and which is upset or confused by theological and political experimentation; and the experimenters need to keep in touch with this great stream, representing so large a part of their own heritage. And within the more experimental forms of Christianity there are immensely important rational and ethical insights whose challenge the conservatives need to hear, and eventually to face, if they are to escape a ghettoed future. Thus dialogue between the two Christianities is quite as important, and might well be both as difficult and as rewarding, as inter-religious dialogue.

74

NOTES

1. See John Bowlby, *Child Care and the Growth of Love*, 2nd ed., Harmondsworth: Penguin, 1965.

2. This view of the fundamental nature of the Christian ethic is presented more fully in the last chapter of my book *Faith and Knowledge*, 2nd ed., London: Fontana paperback, and Cleveland, Ohio: Fountain paperback, 1974.

3. Harvey Cox, *The Secular City*, New York: Macmillan, 1964, and London: SCM Press, 1965.

IV   Christianity and Other Religions

1 *The Christian response to other religions*

Two hundred years ago Fielding's Parson Thwackum could say, 'When I mention religion, I mean the Christian religion; and not only the Christian religion, but the Protestant religion; and not only the Protestant religion, but the Church of England.' Today, however, Christians of different denominations are accustomed to co-operate fully with one another; and they have also become aware that, large though the number of Christians in the world is, an even larger number of people are living by religious faiths other than Christianity. We have visible reminders of this fact in many of our cities now that Hindu and Sikh temples and Muslim mosques have been added to the Jewish synagogues which have long been there. The communities which worship in these places pose new, and to some Christians alarming, questions. Should redundant church buildings be sold to Muslim, Sikh and Hindu congregations who are seeking a place in which to worship? Should religious education in the state schools be exclusively Christian even though a substantial proportion of the pupils in some inner city classes are adherents of other religions? Should national and local religious broadcasting serve the Christian denominations only? In addition to the long-established Councils of Christians and Jews, should we now be developing more Inter-Faiths Councils to include Muslims, Sikhs and Hindus as well?

Behind these practical, and sometimes pressing, issues there lies the fundamental theological question of the Christian attitude to the other world faiths. What positive part is played by those other religions in God's providence? Is there a real problem about this, or can we simply say that the Bible gives them no positive place, and that's that? I think that there is a substantial question here, and that the gradual facing of it within the churches may well bring as big changes in our ways of thinking as did the facing of the fact of biological evolution a century ago. At the moment many are still in the uncomfortable stage of 'not wanting to know'. But this is an inherently unstable state. It cannot be maintained by noting that the Bible only speaks of God's saving activity within Judaic–Christian history, and concluding from this that it is unchristian to think of a world-wide divine initiative towards mankind.

For our distinctive twentieth-century problem in this country arises from rubbing shoulders – literally, in the crowded streets of such cities as London and Birmingham – with men of other faiths of which the biblical writers knew nothing. The Old Testament prophets knew of the savage religions of their primitive neighbours – with children sacrificed on the altar to Moloch – and the early church knew of the now defunct mystery cults of the Roman Empire. But neither Old nor New Testament writers knew of any of the great world faiths beyond Judaism and Christianity. And therefore no application of biblical statements to Islam, Hinduism, Buddhism etc. can possibly claim to represent the original meaning of the texts.

We therefore have to develop a twentieth-century theology of religions in the light of our greatly expanded knowledge of the religious experience of mankind through the ages; for this reveals questions which did not and could not come within the purview of the prophets and apostles of old.

Accordingly our view of the other world religions is today in flux, an earlier consensus having crumbled and a new one having not yet formed. The older consensus was expressed in the traditional Roman Catholic doctrine, 'Outside the Church there is no salvation', and its Protestant missionary equivalent, 'Outside Christianity there is no salvation'. It was in this spirit that the Chicago Congress on World Mission as recently as 1960 declared that 'In the years since the war, more than one billion souls have passed into eternity and more than half of these went to the torment of hell fire without even hearing of Jesus Christ, who He was, or why He died on the cross of Calvary.'[1] But in recent decades other views have replaced this kind of position. The second Vatican Council, in its Declaration on the Relationship of the Church to Non-Christian Religions, said 'The Catholic Church rejects nothing which is true and holy in these religions. She looks with sincere respect upon those ways of conduct and life, those rules and teachings which, though differing in many particulars from what she holds and sets forth, nevertheless often reflect a ray of that Truth which enlightens all men.' And Protestant missionary leaders have been saying rather similar things, as for example in this statement by Canon Max Warren, former General Secretary of the Church Missionary Society: 'When we approach the man of another faith than our own it will be in a spirit of expectancy to find how God has been speaking to him and what new understandings of the grace and love of God we may ourselves discover in this encounter.'[2]

Although the main-line churches have thus abandoned the view of the other world religions as lying outside the sphere of God's grace, they have not yet fully assimilated the implications of their own new attitude. Such a development takes time; and it can be a good method of theological progress for churchmen first to respond with their hearts to the human realities around them, and then gradually to formulate the theological insights implicit in their practical attitudes. The human reality which we in the West have only comparatively recently perceived is that the other world religions have produced equally great saints, mystics and thinkers, and have been sources of spiritual and moral life and orderly frameworks of social existence, for many millions of men and women through many centuries. To dismiss them as inferior now seems dangerously reminiscent of the traditional arrogance of the white man towards the black and brown majority of mankind.

Indeed, whilst theologians have been very good at taking account of all sorts of abstruse or obscure data, they have sometimes failed to notice quite obvious facts which are evident to ordinary people. And one of the things that are obvious to ordinary people, and yet sometimes not regarded by the theologians, is this: that in the great majority of cases – say, 98 or 99% of cases – the religion in which a person believes and to which he or she adheres depends upon where that person was born. That is to say, if someone is born to Muslim parents in Egypt or Pakistan, he or she is very likely to be a Muslim; if to Buddhist parents in Sri Lanka or Burma, a Buddhist; if to Hindu parents in India, a Hindu; if to Christian parents in Europe, North America or Australasia, he or she is very likely to be a Christian. Of course, in each case one may be either an authentic or merely a nominal adherent of one's religion. But if one is born in this country, for example, the religion which one either accepts or rejects will normally be Christianity. If you undergo a religious conversion at the age of seventeen or eighteen, it will in this country normally be a conversion to Christian faith rather than to some other faith. And even if you are a humanist or an atheist, you will be a recognizably Christian one – quite different from, say, a Chinese or a Russian humanist! In short, whether you are a Christian, a Jew, a Muslim, a Sikh, a Hindu, a Buddhist – or for that matter a Marxist or a Maoist – depends nearly always on the part of the world in which you happen to have been born. Any credible religious faith must be able to make sense of this obvious fact. And a credible Christian faith must make sense of it by relating it to faith in the universal sovereignty and fatherhood of God. For we believe that God is the Creator of all mankind, that he has limitless love, and is seeking to save all men and women and not only Christians and their Old Testament spiritual ancestors.

I have introduced the idea of salvation because I take it that this, whatever it is, is the central business of religion: salvation is what religion is all about. What, then, do we mean by salvation? It used to be thought of in Christian theology as a juridical and metaphysical idea: Christ had died for us on the cross, and so now God could justly forgive and accept us. But it is very hard today to make sense of so morally alien an idea. Surely salvation must be thought of more concretely, in terms of the actual quality of human existence. Let us say that God's saving activity is his gradual creating of 'children of God' out of human animals. Salvation consists in human beings becoming fully human, by fulfilling the God-given potentialities of their nature. And this is not a sudden, all-or-nothing affair but a gradual growth, which indeed takes much longer than the span of our life on this earth. Salvation, then, is a slow and many-sided process; and instead of asking of someone, Is he saved? it would be more appropriate to ask, Is he on the way of salvation? Is she becoming more authentically human?

Let us now connect this understanding of salvation with the

problem of other religions. Given a faith in the universal saving activity of God, it is impossible to hold that salvation is only for those living within one particular strand of human history, namely the Judaic–Christian strand. It is impossible to hold that only those born in certain countries in certain periods of history have open to them the possibility of salvation. Such an idea would be neither religiously nor morally supportable. And so theologians have been hard at work, particularly during the last few decades, trying to square their new awareness of God's activity throughout the world and throughout history with traditional Christian beliefs. The point they have mostly reached is a set of variations on the theme that whilst there is salvation within other religions it is all to be seen as the work of Christ. Devout men and women of other faiths are in some hidden but saving sense Christians. The official Roman Catholic way of putting it is in terms of implicit faith: it is not the fault of the deeply religious Muslim, for example, that he has never properly encountered the gospel; but his spiritual state may be such that he *would* respond to it if he encountered it, and in that case he has an *implicit* Christian faith. Karl Rahner has introduced the notion of the 'anonymous Christian'.[3] Devout men and women of other religions are to be regarded as anonymous Christians, and are as such acceptable to God and in the way of salvation. And there are other variations on the same basic theme. What they all amount to, in one form or another, is this – that God is saving men and women within other religions as well as within Christianity; and this is possible because there are men and women within those other religions who are Christians at heart, even if they have never heard the name of Christ. They are anonymous Christians, saved by implicit faith.

Theories of this kind are attempts to achieve two aims which cannot however in the end really be combined. One aim is to retain at the theological level the traditional Christian exclusiveness, the conviction that there is salvation *only* in Christ, and that 'there is no other name under heaven given among men whereby we must be saved' (Acts 4.12, RSV). And the other aim is to acknowledge, at the historical and practical level, that salvation is in fact taking place outside Christianity, and even among people who know little or nothing of Jesus

Christ. It was natural, and indeed perhaps inevitable, that the first phase of our coming to terms with the wider religious life of mankind should be an attempt to have it both ways – by saying that there is salvation only in discipleship to Christ and also that there is salvation outside that discipleship. And in spite of their evident unsatisfactoriness, such moves are to be welcomed. They represent a big step forward from the older assumption that those who are born and die outside Christendom are doomed to forfeit salvation. But nevertheless I do not think that these well-intentioned theories can serve as more than interim measures.

One awkward thing to notice about these ways of granting a secondary kind of validity to the religious life of the non-Christian is that the same device can be adopted by the other religions as well. And there are in fact Hindu philosophers who say that devout Christians are advaita Vedantists at heart, because they have a real desire for the truth although they do not yet know what the truth is. They are anonymous Hindus. And likewise there are Muslim theologians who say that the devout Christian has Islam in his heart and is an anonymous Muslim. But I would suggest that these devices – whether used by Christian, Hindu or Muslim – fulfil the same dubious function as the epicycles with which the old Ptolemaic astronomy was maintained for a little longer before it finally collapsed. The ancient astronomy was based on the dogma that our earth is the centre of the solar system and that the sun and planets revolve around it. This dogma became more and more at variance with increasingly accurate observations of the paths of the planets; and it was only saved by a system of epicycles – imaginary circles centring on the circumferences of other circles, thus forming new and more complex paths which were closer to the actually observed orbits of the planets. And in theory, by postulating ever more complicated arrangements of epicycles, it might have been possible to maintain the Ptolemaic dogma indefinitely. But sooner or later the human mind calls a halt to such an artificial procedure. And so eventually the astronomers were ready for the Copernican revolution from an earth-centred to a sun-centred model of the universe, seeing all the planets, including our own earth, as moving round the sun. This was a breakthrough to a greater realism,

81

in which the highly contrived theory of epicycles was no longer required.

Now it seems to many of us today that we need a Copernican revolution in our understanding of the religions. The traditional dogma has been that Christianity is the centre of the universe of faiths, with all the other religions seen as revolving at various removes around the revelation in Christ and being graded according to their nearness to or distance from it. But during the last hundred years or so we have been making new observations and have realized that there is deep devotion to God, true sainthood, and deep spiritual life within these other religions; and so we have created our epicycles of theory, such as the notions of anonymous Christianity and of implicit faith. But would it not be more realistic now to make the shift from Christianity at the centre to God at the centre, and to see both our own and the other great world religions as revolving around the same divine reality?

2 *Complementary pluralism*

Indeed, if we are to understand the entire range of human awarenesses of the divine, including those enshrined in the Buddhist, Hindu and Taoist, as well as the Christian, Jewish and Muslim traditions, we shall need an even wider framework of thought. Such a framework can perhaps best be approached through a disinction which is found in one form or another within some strand of each of the great traditions. Its Christian form is the distinction between, on the one hand, God as he is in himself, in his infinite self-existing being, independently of and 'before' creation, and on the other hand God in relation to and as experienced by his human creatures. In its Hindu form it is the distinction between Nirguna Brahman, i.e. the absolute Reality beyond the scope of human thought and language, and Saguna Brahman, i.e. Brahman humanly experienced as a personal God with describable characteristics. In Buddhism there is the distinction between the incarnate and the heavenly Buddhas (comprising the Nirmanakaya and the Sambhogakaya), and on the other hand the infinite and eternal Dharmakaya or cosmic-Buddha-nature. Again, the Taoist scriptures begin by saying that 'The Tao that can be expressed is not the eternal Tao'. Within Jewish mysticism (in the *Zohar*) there is the distinction between En Soph, as the infinite divine ground, and the God of the Bible; and within Muslim mysticism (for example, in Ibn Arabi) between Al Haqq, the Real, and our concrete conceptions of God. Likewise, the Christian mystic Meister Eckhart distinguished between the Godhead (*deitas*) and God (*deus*) in a way which closely parallels the Nirguna-Saguna polarity in Hindu thought. And in the present century Paul Tillich has spoken of 'the God above the God of theism'.[4] Contemporary process theology likewise distinguishes between the eternal and temporal natures of God. In all these ways we have a distinction between the infinite transcendent divine Reality *an sich*, or in its/his/her-self, and that same Reality as thought, imagined and experienced by finite human beings.

This distinction enables us to acknowledge both the one unlimited transcendent divine Reality and also a plurality of varying human concepts, images, and experiences of and response to that Reality. These different human awarenesses of and response to the Real are formed by and reciprocally inform the religious traditions of the earth. In them are reflected the different ways of thinking, feeling and experiencing which have developed within the world-wide human family. Indeed these cultural variations amount, on the large scale, to different ways of being human – for example, the Chinese, the Indian, the African, the Semitic, the Graeco-Roman way or ways, and the way of our contemporary technological Atlantic civilization. We do not know at all fully why the life of our species has taken these various forms, though geographical, climatic and economic factors have clearly played their parts.

However, given these various cultural ways of being human we can I think to some extent understand how it is that they constitute different 'lenses' through which the divine Reality is differently perceived. For we know that all human awareness involves an indispensable contribution by the perceiver. The mind is active in perception, organizing the impacts of the environment in ways made possible both by the inherent structure of consciousness and by the particular sets of concepts embedded in particular consciousnesses. These concepts are the organizing and recognitional capacities by which we interpret and give meaning to the data which come to us from outside. And this general epistemological pattern, according to which conscious experience arises out of the interpretative activity of the mind, also applies to religious experience.

The wide range of the forms of human religious experience seems to be shaped by one or other of two basic concepts: the concept of God, or of the Real as personal, which presides over the theistic religions, and the concept of the Absolute, or of the Real as non-personal, which presides over the non-theistic religious hemisphere. These basic concepts do not, however, enter, in these general and abstract forms, into our actual religious experience. We do not experience the presence of God in general, or the reality of the Absolute in general. Each concept takes the range of specific concrete forms which are known in the actual thought and experience of the different religious traditions.

Thus the concept of deity is concretized as a range of divine *personae* – Jahweh, the Heavenly Father, Allah, Krishna, Shiva, etc. Each of these *personae* has arisen within human experience through the impact of the divine Reality upon some particular stream of human life. Thus Yahweh is the face of God turned towards and perceived by the Jewish people or, in more philosophical language, the concrete form in which the Jews have experienced the infinite divine Reality. As such, Yahweh exists essentially in relation to the Hebrews, the relationship being defined by the idea of covenant. He cannot be extracted from his role in Hebrew historic experience. He is part of the history of the Jews, and they are a part of his history. And as such Yahweh is a quite different divine *persona* from Krishna, who is God's face turned towards and perceived by hundreds of millions of people within the Vaishnavite tradition of India. Krishna is related to a different strand of human history from Yahweh, and lives within a different world of religious thought and experience. And each of these divine *personae*, formed at the interface between the divine Reality and some particular human faith community, has inevitably been influenced by human imaginative construction and sinful human distortion as well as by the all-important impact of the transcendent Reality; there is an element of human projection as well as of divine revelation. How otherwise can we account for the ways in which the various divine *personae* have some-times validated cruel massacres, savage punishments, ruthless persecutions, oppressive and dehumanizing political regimes? God, as imaged and understood by the masses of believers within any of the great traditions, must be partly a human construction in order, for example, for God the Father to have been on both sides of the conflict in Europe in the Second World War, and for Allah to have been on both sides of the recent Iraq–Iran conflict. But it does not follow that the divine *personae* are purely human projections. On the contrary, the theory that I am outlining is that they constitute the concrete forms in which the transcendent divine Reality is known to us. Each *is* the Real as perceived and experienced (and partly misperceived and misexperienced) from within a particular strand of the human story.

And essentially the same is to be said concerning the various *impersonae* in terms of which the Real is known in the non-theistic religious traditions. Here the concept of the Absolute is made concrete as Brahman, Nirvana, the Dharma, the Dharmakaya, Sunyata, the Tao. And according as an indivi-dual's thoughts and practices are formed by the advaitic Hindu tradition, or the Theravada or Mahayana Buddhist tradition, he or she is likely to experience the Real in the distinctive way made possible by this conceptuality and meditational discipline.

But can the divine Reality possibly be such as to be authen-tically experienced by millions of people as a personal God, and also by millions of others as the impersonal Brahman or Tao or Sunyata? Perhaps there is a helpful analogy in the principle of complementarity in modern physics. Electromagnetic radia-tion, including light, is sometimes found to behave like waves and sometimes like particles. If we experiment upon it in one way we discover a wave-like radiation, whilst if we experiment upon it in another way we discover a procession of particles. The two observations have both had to be accepted as valid and hence as complementary. We have to say that the electro-magnetic reality is such that, in relation to human observation, it is wave-like or particle-like according to how the observer acts upon it. Analogously, it seems to be the case that when humans 'experiment' with the Real in one kind of way – the way of theistic thought and worship – they find the Real to be personal and when other humans approach the Real in a different kind of way – the way for example of Buddhist or Hindu thought and meditation – they find the Real to be non-personal. This being so, we may well emulate the scientists in their realistic acceptance of the two sets of reports concerning the Real as complementary truths.

Such a theory has the merit that it does not lead us to play down the differences between the various forms of religious experience and thought. It does not generate any pressure to think that God the Father and Brahman, or Allah and the Dharmakaya, are phenomenologically, i.e. as experienced and described, identical; or that the human responses which they evoke, in spiritual practices, cultural forms, life-styles, types of society, etc., are the same. The theory – arrived at inductively by observation of the range of human religious experiences – is that the great world faiths embody different perceptions and conceptions of, and correspondingly different responses to, the Real or the Ultimate from within the major variant cultural ways of being human. Such a theory, I would suggest, does justice both to the fascinating differences between the religious traditions and to their basic complementarity as different human responses to the one limitless divine Reality.

This complementarity is connected with the fact that the great world traditions are fundamentally alike in exhibiting a soteriological structure. That is to say, they are all concerned with salvation/liberation/enlightenment/fulfilment. Each begins by declaring that our ordinary human life is profoundly lacking and distorted. It is a 'fallen' life, immersed in the unreality of *maya*, or pervaded by *dukkha*, sorrow and unsatisfactoriness. But each then declares that there is another Reality, already there and already open to us, in relation to or in identity with which we can find a limitlessly better existence. And each proceeds to point out a path of life which leads to this salvation/liberation. Thus they are all concerned to bring about the transformation of human existence from self-centredness to Reality-centredness. Salvation/liberation occurs through a total self-giving in faith to God as he has revealed himself through Jesus Christ; or by the total self-surrender to God which is *islam*: or by transcending self-centredness and experiencing an underlying unity with Brahman; or by discovering the unreality of the self and its desires and thus experiencing *nirvana*, or by becoming part of the flow of life which in its emptiness-fullness (*sunyata*) is found to be itself *nirvana*. Along each path the great transition is from the sin or error of self-enclosed existence to the liberation and bliss of Reality-centredness.

The true saints (though many different kinds of people have at different times been called saints) are those who are relatively far advanced in this freely-entered transition. Their liberation from self, and thus from grasping for wealth, power and fame, and their re-centring in the divine Reality, have hitherto generally taken two main forms. One is the ascetic form seen in the monastic and the solitary life lived in prayer or meditation. To mention one out of many contemporary examples whom I and others have encountered: Nyanaponika Mahathera, a Buddhist monk who lives in a forest hermitage near Kandy in Sri Lanka, is entirely uninvolved in political and social endeavours, but serves the final Reality by purging away his own self-centredness, by remembering the world in meditation, and by teaching others the methods of self-transcending meditation. The other kind of saint serves the Real by serving his or her fellow human beings in their immediate pain and suffering. One out of many contemporary examples whom I and others have encountered in Kushdeva Singh, a Sikh mystic who is also a physician and a highly practical and creative worker for the sick and dying, for orphans, the poor and the handicapped, in his own city of Patiala in the Punjab. In each case the ordinary human self has become to some real extent transparent to the greater divine Reality in which they rejoice.

But the forms of sainthood vary with the changing shapes of our human situation. Hitherto, sainthood has tended to be non-political and to be expressed in the quality of the individual life and personal relationships. However, in the modern world the establishment of democracy in some countries, and the rising and spreading desire for freedom and for the liberation of the poor, of the black majority of mankind, and of women, from oppressive social structures has opened up new forms of sainthood, of which we see well-known examples in Mahatma Gandhi, Martin Luther King and Camilo Torres. Such political sainthood does not invalidate or replace the older forms, but opens up a third range of vocations within the religious life. There are new paths of self-transcendence today in political and social work, in the preservation of the earth, in working against the threat of thermo-nuclear suicide. And there are many today – dedicated Marxists, socialists, pacifists, environmentalists and others – who have entered upon a way which involves self-giving for the welfare of humanity, but who are entirely secular in their beliefs and who reject all ideas of a transcendent divine Reality. Some of them may well be further advanced in the salvation/liberation transition than others who hold religious beliefs and participate in religious activities but who nevertheless remain firmly centred in themselves. From the religious point of view such secular servants of humanity are involved, without knowing it, in the transition from self-centredness to Reality-centredness; and the religious communities have a mission to show them the further dimension of reality of which they are at present unaware.

3 *The next steps*

What does all this imply concerning the future of religion? Does it point to the formation of a single world religion?

In order to look forward we have first to look back. What we see, from a religious point of view, is that that which we call God has always been present, the divine Spirit ever pressing in upon the human spirit. During what Karl Jaspers has termed the axial period,[5] beginning around 800 BC, great revelatory experiences occurring in different parts of the world gave rise to the different streams of spiritual life which have congealed into what we now know as the world religions. And within all of these, men and women are on the way of salvation by responding to transcendent Reality. But each religion, as an historical entity, is a mixture of the influence of the divine Spirit and of specific human traditions. Within this human element there has, alas, been much evil in the forms of violence and hatred, privilege and oppression, and the authoritarian cramping of the human spirit. And so religions, as historical phenomena, are by no means unambiguously good: each is its own unique mixture of good and evil. And yet each has also provided a home for the human spirit, within which it can grow in grace.

If the divine Logos is indeed at work and has always been at work in this way throughout the life of mankind, we may expect great developments in the various religious traditions in this new age in which they are increasingly interacting with one another. Until recently the religions of the world went their separate ways, wrapped in mutual ignorance. But in this century the world has become a communicational unity, and the scientific study of world religions, inter-faith dialogues and conferences, the experience of religious pluralism in many large cities, have brought us all closer to men of other faiths. The religions of the world have begun to share their insights. For example, Christianity has given something of its social concern to Hinduism; and Buddhism and Hinduism are sharing with the West their vast experience of spiritual meditation. In this larger ecumenical movement the great traditions are coming into a new set of relationships to one another.

Nevertheless the different traditions, embodying their complementary awarenesses of the Real, are likely to continue as distinguishable streams of religious experience and thought, whilst also undergoing some degree of internal change, as long as the human spirit continues to be richly diverse; and we may hope that this diversity will itself continue, ever taking partially new forms, throughout the human future. What is to be desired is not a world-wide uniformity but rather a development in the self-understandings and mutual relationships of the different traditions. Hitherto they have generally seen themselves as existing over against one another as rival religious empires. But as the new idea of complementary pluralism spreads we may expect the different faith communities to come to see themselves and one another somewhat as the different Christian denominations now do – as friends and allies, embodying complementary truths, who remain rivals only in a very qualified and mild sense. For today we no longer, as Methodists, Anglicans, Presbyterians, etc., or even as Roman Catholics, feel that it is religiously essential that all Christians should belong to our own denomination. And the time may well come when we do not as Christians, Muslims, Buddhists, Hindus, etc., feel that it is religiously essential that all human beings should belong to our own tradition. From this point of view the proper understanding of one's own religious faith and commitment in comparison with that of others can be well expressed by adapting a phrase of Rosemary Ruether's. She speaks of her own commitment as a Roman Catholic, rather than as some other kind of Christian, as a matter of 'ecclesial ethnicity' rather than as involving a judgment that her church is objectively superior to all others.[6] Extending the idea, we may say that one's being a Muslim, or a Christian, or a Hindu, etc., is a matter of 'religious ethnicity'. That is to say, Christianity, or Buddhism, or Islam, etc., is the religious community into which one was born, into whose norms and insights one has been inducted, and within which (normally at least) one can therefore most satisfactorily live and grow. There are of course, and will always be, spiritual emigrants; but they are very few in comparison with the vast populations through which each religious tradition is transmitted from generation to generation. And having been born into, say, the Christian religious world one does not have to be able to prove (even to one's own satisfaction) that it is superior to the other religious worlds in order for it to be right and proper for one to be wholeheartedly a Christian. For realistically viewed, one's religious location is usually a matter of 'religious ethnicity' rather than of deliberate and impartial judgment and choice.

The effect of an acceptance of pluralism will not only be to end mutual misrepresentation and communal conflict, but will bring a positive mutual enrichment. Those who accept the pluralist vision are free with good conscience to benefit from the immense spiritual values and insights of other traditions. Thus Christians can learn to practice the profound Hindu methods of meditation, to be fed by the glorious faith of the Muslim Sufis and the Indian *bhaktas*, and to be illuminated by the wisdom of the Buddha, whilst still following Christ as their lord and saviour – that is, the one through whom they have been brought to respond to the divine Reality and to enter upon the great transition from self-centredness to Reality-centredness. And corresponding new possibilities of enrichment likewise open up for the adherents of each of the other great traditions.

But in order wholeheartedly to accept a pluralist understanding of religion, each tradition will sooner or later find that it must develop away from its old assumption of unique possession of the truth and unique superiority as a path of salvation/liberation. Such a development is made possible by the realization in each case that the traditional exclusive claim depends upon a central symbol that is best understood metaphorically, or mythologically, rather than literally. In Hinduism this central symbol is the eternal and absolute character of the Vedas as containing all truth without exception; in Buddhism, the global completeness of the Buddha's insight, so that there can be no other aspects of reality than the *pratitya samutpada* of which he became so vividly aware in his Enlightenment; in Judaism, the absolute character of the Torah, given to God's chosen people; in Islam, the eternal and absolute character of the Qur'an as God's final Word; and in Christianity, the deity of Jesus as the Second Person of the divine Trinity living a human life, so that Christianity alone among the religions was founded by God in person.

Each religious community has to find the right way to use its own mythology. It is not my task as a Christian to tell Buddhists, Muslims or Hindus how to develop their symbol and belief systems in response to their consciousness that their own faith is not the one-and-only but one-among-several. Mutual discussion and criticism are of course possible and helpful within a dialogue in which there is a good basis of trust. But, broadly speaking, religious traditions are changed from within rather than from without, even though the change from within is often a response to what is going on outside. The duty of the religious thinker is to think critically about his own tradition, and to support those within other traditions who are likewise thinking critically, rather than to launch external attacks upon those other traditions. As a Christian theologian I therefore have a vocation to take part in the development of Christian thought. The biggest step in this development is to accept the very idea of development. Christianity has liked to think of itself as unchanging truth flowing down the centuries. But in fact it has (like every other religion) been a continuous history of change. The one abiding factor is our communal memory of Jesus as the man who was so totally open to God that we can see the divine love at work in his life (including his self-giving death and his Easter appearances), and can hear through his words the divine love calling us to open ourselves to God and to be channels of his loving purposes on earth. We have traditionally expressed his significance for us in mythological language by calling him God incarnate, Son of God, etc. But if we treat this symbolic language as literal we shall draw unwarranted inferences from it. And now that God is introducing us, in the 'one world' of today, to his other children we must not be misled into inferring that they are less truly God's children than ourselves, or that he has given them only inferior opportunities to know him and only a second-class status in relation to himself. We are not being unfaithful to the revelation of God's limitless love in Jesus when we see him as constituting a particular disclosure of a universal reality. On the contrary, we are thereby taking the universal reality of God's love seriously.[7]

NOTES

1. *Facing the Unfinished Task*, ed. J. O. Percy, Grand Rapids, Michigan: Eerdmans, 1961, p. 9.

2. M. A. C. Warren in his Introduction to J. V. Taylor, *The Primal Vision: Christian Presence amid African Religion*, London: SCM Press, 1963, p. 10.

3. 'Christianity and the Non-Christian Religions', *Theological Reflections*, Vol. 5, London: Darton, Longman & Todd, and Baltimore: Helicon Press, 1966. See also related essays in *Theological Investigations*, Vols. 6, 9, 12 and 14, and in *God's Word among Men*, ed. G. Gispert-Sauch, Delhi: Vidyajoti, 1973.

4. *The Courage to Be*, New Haven: Yale University Press, 1952, p. 190.

5. Karl Jaspers, *The Origin and Goal of History*, London: Routledge & Kegan Paul, and New Haven: Yale University Press, 1953, chap. 1.

6. *Theologians in Transition*, ed. James M. Wall, New York: Crossroad, 1981, p. 163.

7. This view of the relation between Christianity and other religions is developed more fully in my *God and the Universe of Faiths* (London: Macmillan, and New York: St Martin's Press, 1973), and *God Has Many Names* (London: Macmillan, 1980, and Philadelphia: Westminster Press, 1982). See also *The Experience of Religious Diversity*, ed. John Hick and Hasan Askari (Amersham, Bucks: Avebury Publishing Co., 1983).

V Major Intellectual Difficulties

1 *The challenge of evil*

By evil we mean that which ought not to be – whether human callousness and cruelty; or suffering caused by this or due to disease or accident or natural disaster of some kind; and also the pain suffered by the lower animals. All this confronts us as a problem in two ways. It is a very practical problem with which we all have to grapple at some time, indeed at many times, in our own lives. It is also, when we reflect upon it, a threat to our faith. For even when things are going well with ourselves we know that millions of other people are being assaulted by evil in one form or another and we cannot help asking: why does God allow such things to happen?

Indeed this question probably presents the biggest difficulty there is in the way of a Christian belief in God. Stendhal put the point once and for all when he said: 'God's only excuse is that he does not exist.' In facing this challenge vast issues arise affecting our whole understanding of God and of his purpose in the world. Indeed the challenge goes to the heart of the Christian faith, and any Christian answer must go to the heart of it also.

We must first take our stand with both common sense and the Bible in recognizing that evil really *is* evil – something to be feared, abhorred, resisted and ultimately overcome. This is true both of wickedness and of suffering. Real wickedness exists; we have felt it within ourselves and we have seen it raging in the world. A whole generation of us inevitably think of this in terms of the demonic pitilessness and malevolence that was incarnate in the Nazi attempt to exterminate the Jews from Europe. All of us who lived through those years and who remember the appalling revelations that in 1945 came out of Auschwitz, Belsen, Dachau, Buchenwald and the other concentration camps were shaken to the core by this terrifying unmasking of the implacable contorted face of evil. Again, disease and pain and suffering are not illusions of mortal mind as Christian Science teaches. Nor are they good in disguise. In the earthly work of Christ we see very clearly that disease is contrary to God's will. For Jesus spent his days travelling about Galilee and Judaea healing the sick. God was directly present in those situations; he was not, however, present in the diseases but in Jesus' combating of disease by his healing work. And the same is true in the present day. God is here, not in ills and pains and diseases, but in the work of doctors and nurses and research scientists who are combating these things.

Evil then is unequivocally evil, inimical to good, opposed to God's purpose in his world. It is an enemy, and the biblical writers were so vividly conscious of this that they pictured it in personified form as the Enemy, Satan. But whether evil is personified or not, the question has to be asked, how can a perfectly good and unlimitedly powerful Creator have permitted it to exist?

Christian thinkers have had much to say in face of this challenge. It is often supposed that there is one single form of Christian theodicy – that is, defence of God in face of the evil in his world – so that by this one argument Christianity stands or falls. For example, Bertrand Russell, in his book *Why I am not a Christian*, says: 'The usual Christian argument is that the suffering in the world is a purification for sin.' And he continues, 'I would invite any Christian to accompany me to the children's ward of a hospital, to watch the suffering that is there being endured, and then to persist in the assertion that those children are so morally abandoned as to deserve what they are suffering.'[1]

Russell presumably has in mind here the teaching of Augustine and Thomas Aquinas and the tradition which has followed them that all evil is either sin or suffering incurred as a divine punishment for sin. This tradition does not in fact claim, as Russell suggests, that small children have individually deserved to be punished on account of their own sins but rather that the human race as a whole has become liable to disease and death as a result of a primeval sin. This view does indeed constitute what one might call the majority report of the Christian church on the problem of evil. I shall refer to it as the Augustinian theodicy. But there is also a minority report, representing what I shall call the Irenaean view, after its first major advocate, the second-century theologian Irenaeus.

In its broadest terms the contrast between the two views is this: the Augustinian theodicy seeks its clue to the meaning of evil in the past, in a supposed fall of man at the beginning of history; and so from our standpoint it is a mythological theodicy. The Irenaean view on the other hand looks to the future. It is eschatological, centring on the belief that in the end good will be triumphantly brought out of evil. Its faith is that the eventual fulfilment of God's purpose will be an infinite good in the light of which all that has occurred on the way to it will gain a positive meaning and justification.

The heart of the Augustinian theory is the idea of the fall – that is, basically, the idea that something has gone wrong with a world that was originally wholly good. It follows from this that evil was not created by God but refers rather to a going-wrong, a perversion, a disorder that has come about within the good creation. Evil has no positive existence of its own but is simply a loss or privation or absence of the goodness that something originally had and properly ought to have.

How has this going-wrong occurred within a world that God made wholly good and beautiful? The Augustinian answer is that it has come about through the culpable mis-use by intelligent creatures of the good of moral freedom. On his own relatively lowly level of being man was made wholly good and correspondingly happy; but before the dawn of recorded history he wilfully rebelled against his Creator. This was the fall – the primal crime, a self-destruc-tive rejection of the good which has brought guilt and mis-fortune upon the human race. The fall of man repeated on earth the prior fall of Satan and his angels; and in turn it has brought as its punishment all the natural evils of our human lot – disease and death, earthquakes and storm and drought as well as war, injustice, cruelty, and the other forms of man's inhumanity to man.

This doctrine of the fall provides a theodicy by placing the blame for the origin of evil squarely upon the creature. Before the fall Adam and Eve lived in a paradisal world in perfect contentment, free from any stresses or temptations, and their wilful act of disobedience was therefore inexcusable. It was a crime of virtually infinite malignancy and guilt and one that merited never-ending punishment.

Furthermore, in the Augustinian theodicy, not only is God free from any responsibility for the existence of evil but his purposes are not ultimately threatened or even disturbed by it. For once evil has come about he works it into a larger pattern within which it is made to contribute to the value of the whole. Part of this pattern is formed by the saving of some of those who had fallen, the new and higher good of their redemption justifying the evil of their fall. And for the rest of mankind (traditionally supposed to constitute the majority of the human race) there awaits an eternal punishment which will balance the unlimited evil of their guilt and so restore the moral harmony of the universe. Thus seen in its totality from the divine point of view the universe is perfect in spite of the fact that it contains both sin and suffering.

This great dramatic picture which has dominated the Christian imagination for so many centuries and formed the background to most of the literature and art of the Western world until almost our own time, is open to serious logical, historical, and moral criticisms. The first, most fundamental, criticism is this: the idea of a perfect creation going wrong entirely on its own is self-contradictory. That finitely perfect creatures with no taint of evil in their nature should proceed wilfully to commit sin, would amount to evil creating itself out of nothing. In defence of this paradox Augustinian writers point out that in order to be a creature, and therefore less than God, man must be a limited being; and that in order to be personal he must be genuinely free, and therefore free to choose wrongly. But still, granting this, we must reply that man would never in fact choose wrongly unless there were some flaw either in himself or in his environment. The very fact that he falls shows that he was not finitely perfect after all. Second, the notion that at some point in the distant past the human race consisted of a single pair dwelling in paradisal innocence, and that a first act of rebellion against God brought disease, death, and natural disaster into the world, is incredible in the light of modern knowledge. Third, the idea that God would punish the whole subsequent human race for the disobedience of its first two members attributes to God what to our human understanding can only be called a monstrous injustice. Fourth, the principle that proportionate punishment can rectify the evil of sin and leave the moral perfection of the universe unspoiled is a sub-personal and therefore sub-moral principle which cannot be reconciled with Jesus' vision of God as our heavenly Father.

The Augustinian theodicy therefore involves difficulties just as serious for the twentieth-century Christian as for the twentieth-century agnostic. I believe, however, that there is a viable alternative in the minority report of the Irenaean tradition. The early thinkers of this type, such as Irenaeus himself, shared with their contemporaries the belief in a historical Adam and Eve. But instead of thinking of our first forefathers as finitely perfect and endowed with every grace and virtue they thought of them as immature, or even as children, and as having to undergo a long growth and development before they could reach the state which God had purposed for them; and so their fall was not seen as nearly so grave and catastrophic an event as in the Augustinian tradition. There is in fact here a view of man as still in process of creation and of his perfection as lying before him in the future.

As a theological framework for this Irenaeus distinguished between the 'image' of God in man and the 'likeness' of God in man. The image means man's character as an intelligent social animal, while the likeness represents the eventual perfected human nature which God is seeking to form in us. In modern terms, the first phase of the creative process was the production through the long slow evolution of the forms of life of rational and responsible creatures, made as personal in the image of God. But these are still only the raw material for a further and more difficult stage of the creative process, the leading of men and women through their own free responses into that quality of life which is the finite likeness of God, a likeness which has been revealed to us in the person of Jesus the Christ.

We know today that so long as man has existed as an animal on this earth he has been, in the language of the Genesis myth, a fallen creature – that is to say, centred not upon God in love and glad obedience but upon himself, and necessarily immersed in the hard struggle to survive. He is in this unparadisal state, however, not through having fallen from a prior condition of moral and spiritual excellence but because he was initially brought into being at this distance from human perfection. Accordingly his nature, as a creature still in process of being made and as still involved in what theology calls original sinfulness, is not the result of a primal calamity but represents a stage in God's creative plan.

In this Irenaean type of theodicy our mortality, frailty and vulnerability, within a natural order which is not built so much to comfort as to challenge us, are not a punishment for Adam's sin but a divinely appointed situation within which moral responsibility and personal growth are possible. This world is not intended to be a paradise but a place of soul-making, and the hard demands that it makes upon us are integral to this function. Life requires all the courage, resourcefulness, and skill, and all the compassion and care for one another that men and women can muster; and the uncertainties, the dangers, the obstacles to human purposes through which life makes these demands upon us belong to its God-given character. For in a world without the possibility of real setbacks, frustrations, failures and even disasters our present moral categories would have no meaning. If doing harm to someone is essential to the notion of a wrong action, and if benefiting someone is essential to the notion of a right action, then in a paradise in which there were no such thing as harming or helping there would be no occasion for moral judgment or choice. It would be a world without moral values. For example, the kind of human love that involves mutual support and loyalty and forbearance through the years, and that is often cemented by facing together life's difficulties and disappointments, presupposes something like the kind of imperfect world in which we are living.

But how does soul-making or person-making take place? A divine campaign is now on foot in which we are all called to take part, a campaign of overcoming evil by good. There is a strategy at work of forcing evil, against its nature, to serve indirectly God's purpose of good. Indeed the meaning of our present earthly life lies precisely in this struggle. Within this warfare there is for each a crisis which is traditionally called salvation; and it does not consist in becoming insulated from the world's evil but in enlisting in the campaign to overcome evil with good. As a member of the campaigning army one may in fact be hurt worse than as a neutral civilian; for salvation does not mean to be suddenly made perfect or to be magically protected from all evil but simply to be on the right side in the battle and to know that we shall participate in the final victory.

This divine strategy is often indicated in the Bible. Above all it is shown concretely in the life and death of Jesus. That death is seen there as both the worst and the best thing that has ever happened in human life. It is the worst of evils compelled to serve the supreme good of man's salvation; and as the corruption of the best is the worst, so the redemption of the worst is the best. When we say that Jesus' death was the supreme evil we do not simply mean that it was an unjust and fearfully painful death. In those respects it was far from unique. It was the supremely evil act because it meant the rejection, the most violent and irrevocable possible rejection, of God's love towards us and his claim upon us as these were made real to us by Jesus. Furthermore, this rejection of God was at the same time the rejection of the highest possibility of our own human nature; for we see in Jesus intimations of what we may all ultimately become.

And yet looking back upon the death of Christ across the rich harvest of its effects in human life – a harvest which is reaped anew in each generation – we see a great good drawn by great suffering out of great evil. This rejection, which humanly was so final, has been turned for many into a new beginning. The very violence of the enmity which Jesus met without an answering evil of hatred, has been used to break down the barrier between man and man and between man and God.

We can also look at this event in its place in Jesus' own life and see there a clue to the right attitude to evil. During those last months and weeks as the situation developed, and it became more and more clear that the implacable enmity of the Jerusalem authorities was going to end in his death, Jesus came to see this as an experience which his heavenly Father desired him to undergo for the sake of mankind; and it was his selfless acceptance of it that has made it a means to man's salvation. The spirit in which he faced suffering made it a redemptive suffering, an overcoming of evil by good. This attitude of Jesus has been in the pattern of the Christian response to suffering ever since. That is to say, suffering is not sent or planned by God, as Jesus' death was not planned or engineered by God. Such things are caused by human malevolence or by harsh aspects of the world in which we live. The suffering they cause is not good but evil. Nevertheless when the evil situation has come about, and the practical question is how to react to it, there are always two different ways open to us. We can close ourselves up in bitterness and resentment so that our suffering becomes an ever thickening wall between ourselves and God. Or we can trust in the God whom Jesus trusted. Then although we cannot turn the evil to good by our own power we may nevertheless so react as to allow good to be brought out of it in the end.

The pain, the disease, the disaster, the failure, the humiliation, the suffering, the guilt, the sorrow of human life is not itself good and does not itself become good. But nevertheless it can be *used* for good; and to try so to use it is the way of Christian faith. This is easy to say but not easy to practice. But that it can be practised is proved again and again by those who have been seen practising it – people who amid hardship have found strength of character; who in crises have become competent to help others; who even in bereavement or in the time of their own approaching death have become luminously conscious that God is present with them.

But if we look at this world in this way, as a place of soul-making, we cannot avoid noticing how extremely ambiguous it is and how utterly uncertain its success. Sometimes indeed obstacles breed strength of character, dangers evoke courage and unselfishness, and calamities produce patience and moral steadfastness. But sometimes they lead instead to resentment, fear, grasping selfishness and tragic disintegration of character. Life can be soul-destroying as well as soul-making. And therefore this type of theodicy, which finds its clue to the meaning of evil in God's eventual decisive bringing of good out of it, is driven to look beyond this world and to take seriously the Christian hope of eternal life. This aspect of Christianity tends to be soft-pedalled nowadays, presumably because it makes such an openly transcendent claim. But no theodicy is possible without such a claim. For if human personality becomes extinct at the moment of bodily death then a great part of the evil of this world must remain for every unjustified.

Millions of people in each generation over the hundreds of thousands of years during which man has existed have had to live stunted lives in desperate poverty, or as physically incomplete beings or as congenital mental defectives, or have been killed in unfulfilled youth by war or famine or disease; and for many of these millions this life can only be regarded as tolerable if it leads on to another and better life. If it remains a preparation for something that will never happen then it is a cruel mishap indeed. But, on the other hand, if in the end the human individual is to be brought through a process of soul-making continued in other spheres beyond this world to the perfection intended for him by God, then the meaning of this present life is transformed for those who suffer and is enhanced for those for whom it is already good. For the end towards which it is moving is an infinite because eternal good which is able to justify all that has been endured on the way to it. The main New Testament symbol for this end is the kingdom of God. It is in other words a community – a community whose life is an ever-new experience of the infinitely manifold goodness of the Creator.

Such a theodicy, pointing to the ultimate fulfilment of God's good purpose for his creatures, is only consistent if it affirms the eventual salvation of all men. The traditional alternative to this in the doctrine of eternal punishment entails the permanent reality of evil in the forms of perpetual sin and perpetual suffering. And accordingly modern Irenaean thinkers have generally rejected the doctrine of hell. Even the much milder possibility that lost souls might simply fade out of existence would entail that God's purpose for them is finally frustrated.

So far I have been contrasting these alternative responses to the problem of evil. Yet despite these large differences there is also a hidden convergence between the two types of theodicy. Officially the fundamental issue between them concerns God's responsibility for the existence of evil. The ostensible aim of the Augustinian tradition is to preserve the Creator from any such responsibility by heaping it without remainder upon the creature. But in practice this aim is undermined by a doctrine of divine predestination according to which God has destined some for salvation and others for damnation. At the human level it is still the fault of sinners that they sin, for they do so of their own free will. But at the same time God created them in the knowledge that they would freely sin and with the decree hanging over them that having sinned they were to be damned. This doctrine implies an ultimate divine responsibility, not in the sense that God is answerable to anyone, but in the sense that his decision to create as he did was a necessary precondition of all that has happened, including human sin and suffering, and that he acted in full knowledge of what would result. And so the Augustinian theodicy implies, even if it does not openly affirm, a divine omni-responsibility.

The alternative Irenaean type of theodicy has been more ready to say explicitly that God, as the sole Creator and Ruler of the universe, bears the ultimate responsibility for it. For there is no one else to share that final responsibility; and it is perhaps as presumptuous as it is ineffectual for theologians to attempt to relieve God of it by taking it upon mankind. Our trust has to be wholly in God, who is not an irresponsible Creator but the loving Father in whose presence we can know that 'all shall be well, and all shall be well, and all manner of thing shall be well.'[2]

2 Conflict with modern science?

It is a very familiar truth that our modern world – using this phrase with the parochial meaning of Europe and North

American since about 1500 – has been increasingly transformed by a continuing scientific revolution which includes within it the industrial revolution of the nineteenth century and the technological revolution of the twentieth century. The outcome at the present time is a world which would have seemed to our ancestors of only a few generations ago to be a place of magic and fantasy – in which men fly through the sky in great heavier than air machines, speak across thousands of miles, are seen in distant towns on a screen; in which machines work by the unseen power of electricity and houses and towns are brightly lit at night; in which computers multiply indefinitely the calculating power of the human brain; in which many diseases which were then normally fatal are now normally curable; in which the expectation of life has been almost doubled (from about thirty-six years in Europe in the eighteenth century to seventy years for men and about seventy-four years for women today); but in which also there are weapons so powerful that a thermonuclear war would destroy scores, perhaps hundreds, of millions of people.

In transforming the conditions of human life, the development and application of scientific knowledge has also transformed the ways in which men think. In a time of ignorance concerning the workings of nature, phenomena whose causes were not understood could readily be attributed to supernatural agencies. And so if there was a drought and the crops were failing, or storms and floods threatened a village, or the plague was approaching, prayer seemed an appropriate way of trying to avert the danger. Today we still suffer from droughts, floods and epidemics, but we also know a good deal about their causes and their remedies; and although we are still not always able to provide the necessary irrigation, drainage, sanitation, inoculation, etc., we know that these operate in exactly the same way whether prayer is resorted to or not.

Generalizing, what mankind has discovered – though of course it no longer comes to us as a discovery but as a familiar and obvious fact – is that nature forms an integral system exhibiting its own causal regularities such that to know these laws is to be able to some extent to divert the course of nature for human ends. Superhuman personal powers – deities, angels, devils, spirits – form no part of the field of forces which science explores. Scientific research makes no use of the concept of the supernatural and the question of the existence of God is simply irrelevant to the development and validation of scientific theories.

This conclusion, which now operates in the minds of mid-twentieth-century Western theologians as much as of other mid-twentieth-century men and women, took roughly the hundred years prior to the first World War to be effectively established. During that century of intermittent controversy between science and religion the main issue was the challenge of the theory of evolution to the biblical accounts of the age of the world, the origin of man and his relation to the animal kingdom and, by implication, to the reliability of the Bible as a source of knowledge on subjects that come within the province of the natural sciences. The pattern that we now see as we look back upon the nineteenth century is one of steadily advancing scientific discovery – particularly as regards the age of the earth and the evolution of the forms of life upon it – matched by steadily retreating religious dogmatism. When the geologists learned that the earth must be thousands of times older than the approximately six thousand years of the biblical chronology, most theologians and ecclesiastics resisted the evidence, believing that they were thereby defending the truth of the Bible. When Darwin's theory of natural selection offered a detailed account of the process whereby the forms of life have evolved over immense periods of time from the amoeba to man the general ecclesiastical response was to resist the new theory, again in the interests of the truth of the book of Genesis and thus of the Bible as a whole. Many doughty champions of biblical inerrancy were unable to come to terms with the new knowledge and had to leave it to their successors to abandon the biblical chronology and the special creation of man and his distinction from the animal kingdom, and then to go on to accept the idea of a universal causal system of nature which challenges the whole mythical and miraculous thought world of the biblical writings.

Today the contemporary mind, formed under the impact

of the practical and theoretical success of the sciences, assumes that the physical universe is explicable without reference to supernatural agencies; and furthermore that any credible religious faith must be compatible with this principle. For those who share this outlook the important theological question has become whether Christianity is or is not compatible with the basic scientific assumption of the autonomy of nature.

There is here a parting of the ways between two conceptions of Christianity. One is a hangover from the medieval Europe whose cultural assumptions it preserves; and this understanding of Christianity is not compatible with the methodological presuppositions of modern science. The other represents a development of Christian thought which was impossible within the medieval world but which has now been made possible by the growth of a powerful scientific culture. According to this latter view the physical universe is a divine creation, determined by a purpose which has deliberately made it an autonomously functioning sphere in which its Creator is not evident. For while the physical universe may serve many other ends which do not concern the human race, its function in relation to ourselves is to enable finite personal life to exist in its own creaturely world. The Creator is so disproportionate to his creatures, as the infinite Being over against finite beings, that the two cannot exist in the same sphere. If they were to run on the same rails of physical existence there would be no room left for the creature! Therefore God, who is not a physical entity but Spirit, has created man within and as part of a physical universe in which he can live his own proper creaturely life. For only if man is a free being existing in his own sphere at a distance from his Creator can he make a free response of faith and worship to that Creator. The 'distance' from himself at which God has created man is not, however, a spatial distance; spatially the infinite Being cannot be at a distance from anything or anyone. It is an epistemic distance, a distance in the dimension of knowledge, consisting in the fact that we do not automatically know God. His existence is not involuntarily evident to us; and therefore it is possible for us to *come* to know him. (This same point has been made, on pp. 46–48 and 56, in connection with religious faith.)

Now the character of the universe in virtue of which it constitutes an autonomous natural environment for man is also its character as a causally law-abiding realm in which man himself has emerged within and as part of the world process. It is because we can explain the world and our existence within it without God that we have an epistemic freedom in relation to him.

This then is the new picture of the relation between science and religion, which theology offers: we exist by God's creative action as parts of a universe which constitutes an autonomous order; and the sciences are the activities in which we systematically explore and to some extent come to control this order from within. it. There is no conflict between science and religion, for any development of scientific knowledge describing the natural order more and more fully without reference to God is compatible with the belief that God has deliberately created a universe in which he is not compulsorily evident but can be known only by a free personal response of faith.

I think it must, however, be added that if one exercises one's imagination sufficiently ingeniously one can conceive of scientific discoveries which, while still logically compatible with the truth of religion, would nevertheless in practice lead most believers to abandon or radically alter their convictions. For example, suppose it were established that religious belief was exactly correlated with the level of some isolable chemical substance in the bloodstream. By injecting this substance into him an atheist could be turned into a believer and by neutralizing it a believer could be turned into an atheist – so that conversion and deconversion could be offered in a clinic. This would lead us to think of the religious state of mind very much as we now think of the psychedelic state. That is to say, it may or may not be desirable but it is presumed not to be an awareness of the true character of the universe; it is assimilated to the fantasies of the dissociated mind rather than to the intuitions of a cognitive genius such as Newton or Einstein.

There is then a theoretical possibility of conflict between

106

scientific discoveries and religious convictions; and indeed that there is this possibility supports the theologian's insistence, to be discussed in the following section, upon the factual (i.e. factually true-or-false) character of the system of religious assertions. But the theoretical possibility of conflict is not an actual conflict. The present state of scientific knowledge offers no opposition to the claims of religion when these latter are rightly formulated.

Let us test this thesis in relation to the idea of the creation of the universe by a transcendent God. In scientific cosmology there have in recent years been two rival theories of the origin of the universe. The starting-point of both theories is the fact that the universe is expanding. This is inferred from analysis of the light from very distant stars, whose rays show a shift towards the red end of the spectrum, indicating movement away from us. According to the 'steady-state' theory the universe has existed in more or less its present form through unlimited time without having ever had a beginning. The continuous expansion of the universe has not led to a given region of space becoming depopulated of galaxies because the scattering effect is being compensated by a continuous creation of new matter evenly throughout space in the form of thin hydrogen gas which eventually condenses into new galaxies. As a result there is a more or less constant population of galaxies within a given radius from us. This continuous creation of matter has been going on *ad infinitum* and therefore no initial state of the universe needs to be postulated.

However, more recent observations have convinced most astronomers that the rival 'big bang' theory is more likely to be correct. According to this theory the matter composing the universe was at one time in a state of maximum density and at a moment which is roughly calculated as some fifteen thousand million years ago it 'exploded', beginning an accelerating expansion which is still taking place around us.

For our present purpose the important point is that neither of these theories has either theological or antitheological significance, in spite of the fact that one theory speaks of the continuous creation of matter out of nothing and the other of an initial state of the universe a roughly computable number of years ago. For the continuous creation of hydrogen, formerly postulated by Fred Hoyle and others, was not meant to imply a Creator; the steady-state theory treated the appearing of hydrogen atoms uniformly in space and time as an ultimate given characteristic of the universe. And the big bang or instantaneous creation of G. Gamow's theory is not to be identified as an absolute beginning; it may only represent a point in an eternal series of alternate expansions and contractions. Neither theory, then speaks of creation in the absolute sense required in theology; and yet each is compatible with the theological claim that the universe, whatever its mode of being, is a divine creation.

It should be added that the sciences are themselves in process of continuous expansion; so that the question of their relationship to religion has to be kept under constant review. For example, very recent observations and arguments in astrophysics are now tending away from the oscillating model for the universe and towards the idea that the 'big bang' was an absolute beginning.[3]

But does not the idea of divine creation entail that the universe had a beginning in time, however long ago, and is it not thus incompatible with any cosmological theory which assumes that the universe has always existed? Certainly many religious thinkers have taken this view. But a different possibility was propounded in the fourth century AD by St Augustine (*City of God*, xi, 6) when he suggested that the universe was not created *in* time, so that one could ask what was happening before the moment of creation, but that time is itself an aspect of the created universe. Space-time does not exist or occur in time, for time is a dimension of it. If this is so it may also be, as relativity theory suggests, that space-time is internally infinite – that is to say from within the space-time continuum the universe is found to be unbounded both spatially and temporally. In that case it has had no initial state. But it may nevertheless, while internally infinite, depend for its existence and its nature upon the will of a transcendent God.

This latter is the essence of the religious doctrine of creation: namely, that the universe as a spatio-temporal whole exists in virtue of its relation to God. We have, however, no non-temporal language in which to express this relationship. If we say that God willed the universe, or that he holds and will continue to hold it in existence, we are using verbs in the past, present and future tenses. But the relation between Creator and creature, although describable from the standpoint of the creature in terms of temporal activity, must from the standpoint of the Creator be a non-temporal relationship; and yet a relationship to temporal beings through whose experience God also participates in temporality.

The relation between time and eternity involved in the idea of divine creation is one of the most difficult of concepts to deal with; but the point which I am seeking to make here is simply that the religious notion of creation is neither confirmed by nor in conflict with theories and discoveries in scientific cosmology.

3 *The problem of verification*

The prolonged discussions among philosophers, especially during the 1930s, about the idea of verification have left an important legacy with us today. In particular they have thrown a definitive light on the concept of factual assertion, even though our notions of it are now much broader than those being mooted a generation ago. The permanent gain secured by pre-war logical positivism is that it has made us realize that the ideas of fact and existence are closely bound up with the idea of making an experienceable difference. It is a question of fact whether it is now raining in Birmingham if it makes an experienceable difference whether it is now raining in Birmingham. And that X exists means that the universe differs in some experienceable particular from the way it would be if there were no X. In short, we may say that in order to constitute a factual assertion a proposition must be such that it makes an experienceable difference whether it be true or false. Any state of the universe that satisfies the proposition in question must differ in an appropriate way from any state of the universe that fails to satisfy it. If it makes no difference at all in the past, present or future, whether an apparent assertion is true, then we must say that it is not a factual assertion; it lacks cognitive or descriptive meaning.

This is intended as a non-controversial statement. In spite of that it creates a major problem for theology. Of course in a broad sense of 'theological' there are many theological utterances which qualify without difficulty as factual – for instance, such historical statements as that in the first half of the first century AD, in what is today Israel, Jesus lived and died and was believed by his followers to have risen from the dead. But there are others that are theological in the narrower sense of being about God: for instance, 'God created the universe out of nothing' and 'God loves mankind'. For Christianity these are central statements. It is from their connection with these that the historical propositions of theology receive their religious significance. And although such core statements have the form of factual assertions, their status is nevertheless open to question. The challenge is to show that they are genuine assertions, propositions concerning which a truth-claim can be lodged and considered.

What experienceable difference, then, does it make whether there is a God who has created the universe and who loves mankind? The question could be answered either by saying how the world would be different if this were not so or by saying what future events would serve to confirm that it is so.

Someone might say: 'It makes literally *all* the difference whether God exists; for if he had not created the universe there would not now be a universe – and that is as massive a difference as one could ask for!' But it is too big a difference for our present purpose. We are seeking a difference *within* human experience; and the non-existence of the entire universe could not be an object of human experience since there would be no human beings to experience it.

Someone else might say: 'The difference lies within the religious believer himself. It consists in his vivid consciousness of living in the presence of God.' This is the kind of experience I have described in chapter II (see pp. 42f., 50f.), saying that for the religious man it may sometimes have as compelling a quality as his sense experience. It cannot at such times be other than sufficient for him, and therefore it cannot leave open for him the question whether God exists nor (if it should be raised) the philosophical question whether there can be factual assertions about God. The man of faith, then, needs no further confirmation of God's reality.

But this fact does not meet the problem raised by the contemporary philosophical enquirer. His question can be asked even after he has noted that some people claim to have a vivid consciousness of God. He wants to know whether the existence of God makes any further and less private and subjective difference. Does the Christian's faith involve the expectation of any more public confirmation? Can a critic, examining the system of Christian beliefs, see that whether or not these are true they are at any rate genuinely factual beliefs, liable to be either verified or falsified within human experience?

Although the system of Christian beliefs is not as a whole directly verifiable, is there perhaps some one aspect of it which is in principle experientially confirmable and which can establish the factual character of the other beliefs that are bound up with it? There are certain eschatological expectations – expectations about the ultimate future – which, I want to suggest, satisfy an acceptable criterion of factual meaningfulness and which impart to the Christian belief-system as a whole the character of a true or false assertion.

Let me first put the situation in terms of a parable, inspired by Bunyan's *Pilgrim's Progress*. Two men are travelling together along a road. One of them believes that it leads to the Celestial City, the other that it leads nowhere; but since it is the only road there is they must both travel it. Neither has been this way before and neither can say what they will find round each next corner. During their journey they meet both with moments of refreshment and delight and with moments of hardship and danger. All the time one of them, Mr Christian, thinks of his journey as a pilgrimage to the Celestial City and experiences the pleasant stretches as encouragements and the obstacles as trials of his purpose and lessons in endurance prepared by the King of the City to make of him a worthy citizen when at last he arrives there. The other, Mr Humanist, believes none of this and sees their journey as an unavoidable and ultimately aimless ramble.

Since he has no choice in the matter he enjoys the good and endures the bad. But for him there is no Celestial City to be reached, no all-encompassing purpose ordaining their journey, but only the road itself and the luck of the road in good weather and in bad.

Now during the course of the journey the issue between them is not an experimental one. They do not have different expectations about the coming details of the road but only about its ultimate destination. And yet when they do turn the last corner it will be apparent that one of them has been right all the time and the other wrong. So although the issue between them has not been able to be settled by experiment yet it has nevertheless from the start been a real issue. They have not merely felt and talked differently about the road: one of them was feeling and talking in a way that was appropriate and the other in a way that was inappropriate to the actual state of affairs. Their opposed interpretations of the road constituted genuinely rival assertions, though assertions whose assertion-status has the unusual characteristic of being guaranteed retrospectively by a future crux.

This is peculiar enough; but it must be admitted that it is not the only peculiarity in the idea of an eschatological verification of Christian faith. Indeed the very idea of taking eschatology seriously enough to rest anything important upon it is peculiar today. It has been said, and it may well be true, that the belief in an after-life is no longer part of the effective convictional system even of the majority of professing Christians. Nevertheless it plays a prominent part in the teaching of Jesus and it connects, I am suggesting, with our contemporary philosophical understanding of the nature of a factual assertion. Accordingly the theologian may properly draw upon this particular aspect of the Christian tradition to establish that the claims of Christianity are genuinely factual claims.

But has not the notion of an after-life been ruled out by modern philosophers? The answer is that it is ruled out by some and not by others; and these latter include some of the most strongly science-oriented thinkers. For example Moritz Schlick, who was at the centre of the Vienna Circle from which logical positivism originally emanated, held that the hypothesis that after death I shall continue to have conscious experiences is an empirical hypothesis. Schlick did not at all think that there *is* an after-life, but he acknowledged that the statement that there is a genuinely factual assertion.[4]

If Schlick and others are right about this, as I think they are, the next peculiarity is that the belief in an after-life is one which will be verified in human experience if it is true but which cannot be falsified in human experience if it is false. For if we live after our bodily death we shall (presumably) know that we have survived death; but if not we shall never know that we have not survived it – for we shall not be there to know anything. This characteristic of being verifiable if true, but not falsifiable if false, distinguishes the expectation of a life after death from an ordinary scientific hypothesis. For as Karl Popper has argued (in *The Logic of Scientific Discovery*)[5] a scientific hypothesis is useful precisely because it is in principle falsifiable; it is deliberately so formed that if it is mistaken it can sooner or later be shown to be mistaken. But the survival hypothesis is not constructed in this way. Another and even larger point of difference is that whereas a hypothesis in the physical sciences is required to be verifiable or falsifiable in *sense* experience – by looking at pointer readings and so on – experiences after death cannot be bodily experiences in the same sense. It should, however, be added that the Judaic-Christian doctrine of the resurrection of the body – which does not, in the thought of St Paul, for example, mean the resuscitation of corpses but the divine reconstitution of the human personality in both its inner and outer aspects – allows in its own way for bodily experiences in the new life beyond the grave (on this see pp. 109f.).

However, the chief difficulty does not lie in the points I have mentioned so far. It lies in the task of specifying the character of an after-life that would confirm the central Christian claims concerning the reality and love of God. For the bare fact of a continued post-mortem existence would not serve to establish anything of distinctively religious concern. The universe could conceivably be such that human personality survives death but such that our endless existence neverthless has no purpose or goal or final meaning. And in that case the claims of Christianity would be false.

113

If after-death experiences are to count as confirming the distinctively Christian claims about the nature and governance of the universe, they must render it not only rational to believe in the God of Christian faith but irrational not to. The ambiguities of our present life must be transcended in a situation which is wholly evidential of the reality and love of God. This would be the situation to which the New Testament points under the symbol of the kingdom of God. Whereas our present world is ambiguous, in some ways suggesting a divine Creator and in other ways suggesting the contrary, the symbol of the kingdom points to a future in which God's rule will be directly evident and in which all things will reflect the divine goodness. The world will be transparent to its Creator. In such a situation it would still not indeed be possible in any literal sense to *see* God, despite the traditional doctrine of the Beatific Vision, for he is not a visible object. But it would be possible to see and indeed impossible not to see our environment as directly expressing God's presence and love: in this sense human beings would 'see' God.

Now the trouble is that while one can speak of such a state of affairs in these very general terms one cannot specify it much further. Indeed if there is a God he has ordained that we should not be able to look beyond this life and has insured that any

> Tales and golden histories
> Of heaven and its mysteries

can only be products of the poetic imagination. We are required to live within the limitations and on the time scale set for us by the fact of inevitable bodily death.

Still, the dimly imaginable fulfilment of God's purpose for us beyond our earthly mortality remains an indelible part of the Christian message; and it is permissible to think speculatively in response to the questions that it inevitably provokes. The special problem confronting the notion of eschatological verification is this: how are we to postulate sufficient correlation between the Christian's present expectations and a future situation of unambiguous divine rule, in view of the admitted vagueness of these expectations?

How could a heavenly world be recognized as confirming Christian faith?

The basic connection has to be with our present awareness of living in the unseen presence of God – or with an awareness which arises beyond this life, at a later stage of our journey towards the eschatological situation. In the present world this awareness occurs in tension with many contradicting circumstances – all the many forms of suffering, depravity, ugliness and decay. But in the eschatological state there will be no such contradicting circumstances. Everything will accord with our sense of trusting in the divine presence and being within the sphere of the loving divine purpose. One aspect of this will be the perfecting of our own nature. We cannot now concretely visualize this perfection, even though we glimpse aspects of it in all that is best in human life. But the fact that we cannot now describe it does not necessarily mean that the situation itself would not be identifiable by one who participates in it. A little child is unable to conceive what it will be like to be grown up; but as he grows, his understanding of adulthood also grows, so that he has no difficulty in recognizing that state when he has reached it. And the fulfilment of God's purpose for mankind may be as remote from our present human condition as is adult maturity from the mind of a baby. But any development towards it will involve a growing appreciation of the nature of that fulfilment, so that the problem of recognition will disappear in the process.[6]

NOTES

1. Bertrand Russell, '*Why I am not a Christian*' *and Other Essays on Religion and Related Subjects*, ed. Paul Edwards, London: Allen & Unwin, 1957, p. 22; New York: Simon & Schuster, 1957, pp. 29f.

2. Mother Julian of Norwich, *The Relevations of Divine Love*, trans. by James Walsh, London: Burns & Oates, 1961, New York: Harper & Row, 1962, ch. 27, p. 92. I have written more fully about the problem of evil in *Evil and the God of Love*, 2nd ed., London: Macmillan, and New York: Harper & Row, 1977.

3. See e.g. J. R. Gott, G. E. Gunn, D. N. Schramm and B. M. Tinsley, 'An Unbound Universe?', *The Astrophysical Journal*, Vol. 194.3, 1974, pp. 543ff.; A. Sandage and G. A. Tammann, 'Steps toward the Hubble Constant, VI', *The Astrophysical Journal*, Vol. 197.2, 1975, pp. 265ff.

4. Moritz Schlick, 'Meaning and Verification', *The Philosophical Review*, Vol. 45, July 1936, pp. 339–69.

5. Karl Popper, *The Logic of Scientific Discovery*, London: Hutchinson, and New York: Basic Books, 1959.

6. I have further developed and defended the idea of eschatological verification in *Faith and Knowledge*, 2nd ed., London: Fontana paperback, and Cleveland, Ohio: Fountain paperback, 1974.

VI The Future

1 *Life and death*

Christians believe that we human beings are living a double life – a mortal life and, overlapping and interpenetrating it, an eternal life. This Christian claim is certainly a tremendous one, not only hard to believe but also hard to understand. And yet even apart from any religious teaching it is clear that we do have a double status which is unique among the creatures of this world. On the one hand we are animals, formed out of the long slow evolutionary process. We have emerged out of the lower forms of life and we constitute part of the continuous realm of nature. And as animals we are mortal, made (as the book of Genesis says) out of the dust of the earth and destined to return to that dust. We have a normal life span today, in the more affluent countries, of some seventy years. And then in our seventies or our eighties or at most our nineties we shall die, and this living body, then lifeless and cold, will begin to disintegrate and return to the dust of the earth. This on the one hand is true.

But on the other hand while we are part of nature, in a quite precise sense we transcend nature. For we are possessed of reason, which is the power to contemplate and understand nature, including our own nature, from an intellectual vantage point outside it. As physicists and chemists, astronomers and cosmologists, psychologists, sociologists and historians, as poets and philosophers we transcend the natural order of which we are a part. For while the physical universe goes blindly on its way in a stream of unconscious cause and effect, we are centres of self-consciousness and freedom. Around these centres there has developed a moral conscience and a sense of values and of responsibility in virtue of which we are rational and moral persons. And Christianity adds that as such we are made in the image of God as beings to whom he can give eternal life.

For the teaching of Jesus includes as an essential element the affirmation of life after death. That our life is renewed beyond death because God's graciousness to us has an absolute and therefore an eternal quality was for him one of the basic facts in terms of which we have to live. And if we trust what Jesus said out of his own direct consciousness of God we shall share his belief in the future life. This belief is supported by the reasoning that a God of infinite love would not create finite persons and then drop them out of existence when the potentialities of their nature, including their awareness of himself, have only just begun to be realized.

Jesus did not, however, indicate the mode of the afterlife – whether embodied or disembodied and, if embodied, in what kind of material. Subsequent discussions suggest that two rather different conceptions of the life to come are possible on the basis of Jesus' teaching and that a choice between them depends more upon philosophical than upon strictly religious considerations. Today when we are conscious as seldom or never before of the tentative, provisional and always reformable character of theological work it is appropriate to keep all options open – which in the present case means developing both conceptions of the after-life instead of dogmatically sponsoring one and excluding the other. I shall describe them both here, necessarily only in brief outline, without feeling it necessary to attempt to decide between them.

One of these possibilities, and the one which is closer to the thought-world of the Bible, is the idea of the resurrection of the body. Given the basic religious conviction that the eternal love of God bestows immortality upon its objects, the doctrine of resurrection arises from the view of man which operates throughout most of the Bible, the view in which the human being is not divided into a material body and immaterial soul. For the writers of the Bible man's spirituality is neither contrasted with nor separated from his materiality. Rather his spirituality is a material spirituality and his materiality is a spiritual materiality. This view is in line with our prevailing contemporary scientific and philosophical conception of the human being as a psycho-physical unity. The mind is indissolubly connected with the brain so that the death of the one is also the death of the other. And for the same reason the reconstitution of the one would be the reconstitution (or 'resurrection') of the other.

This reconstitution was at one time generally thought of, and is perhaps even now sometimes thought of by simple souls, as the literal resuscitation to physical life of corpses raised from their graves. Such a notion is of course grotesque and is indeed hardly capable of being visualized in detail. (It provokes unanswerable conundrums such as, what happens to the eye which has been transplanted immediately after death into a blind person, enabling him to see? Or the leg eaten by a shark in the Pacific thirty years before the death of the rest of the body – which by then has, probably, become entirely composed of different matter?) However, in the only explicit discussion of the subject in the New Testament, which is the fifteenth chapter of St Paul's first Letter to the Corinthians, the resurrection of the dead has no such crude physical meaning. St Paul says that there is a spiritual body (*soma pneumatikon*) as well as an animal body (*soma psychikon*).

One possible development of this idea is that at death the living psycho-physical unity is totally extinguished, but at that moment or some moment thereafter God creates a psychomaterial replica – a complete bodily structure including the brain with all its memory traces – which is the resurrected person. The resurrection world, or universe of worlds, inhabited by resurrected persons is accordingly spatial, but its space is a different space from that in which we now are. That is to say no position in one universe is at any distance or in any direction from any position in the other. Nevertheless there is full continuity of personal identity between a living person in this world and his replica in the resurrection world, for there is continuity of both bodily and mental characteristics including memory. This provides the basis for a conception of the resurrection of the dead.

The other possible fulfilment of the teaching of Jesus concerning life after death is based upon the claim, for which there is some evidence, that consciousness can in fact exist apart from the body including the brain and central nervous system. There is evidence in the phenomena of extra-sensory perception of mental activity which is not physically mediated; and there is even evidence which is not lightly to be dismissed, though it is difficult to assess, of continued consciousness and memory after physical death, in some of the mediumistic phenomena such as cross-correspondences and other apparent communications from the 'dead'.[1]

These indications of the autonomy of mental life have suggested to some contemporary philosophers who have taken account of the evidence of psychical research or parapsychology an hypothesis[2] which has an affinity with the ancient Hindu conception of *kama loka* ('the world of desire'). According to this theory the post-mortem environment is plastic to the mind, being mental rather than material in nature. It is mind-dependent, its content being provided by memories retained from our present embodied life (perhaps including now unconscious memories) moulded by our desires. It is in fact from our present embodied point of view a dream-like world formed by the power of wish fulfilment. However, although produced by the mental mechanism which creates dreams, this other world is entirely real in the experience of those whose world it is. For example, in it one has a body – that is to say one has sensations and images like the sensations and images that we now receive from our bodies. It is, moreover, a stable objective environment based upon the structure of our character, which changes only slowly; and it operates according to its own laws, which are probably more like those of Freudian psychology than of physics. It is also a world that is common to a community of people – those who share sufficiently similar desires and thoughts. Indeed there may well be many worlds, perhaps some quite distinct from one another and some partially or occasionally overlapping, so that, for example, Socrates and Spinoza may inhabit a common world which may, however, be quite separate from that inhabited by Genghis Khan and Hitler. The web of communication by which a number of people are conscious of the same environment is telepathic. The telepathic interaction of minds creates correlated sensory images so that each individual has appropriate experiences of seeing, hearing, touching, etc., just as in our present life.

In short the next world or worlds will be a real environment in which life really continues. But it continues with a major difference. The principle of judgment, or in Eastern terms *karma*, which has been largely postponed in its operation in our present life by a material world which is not immediately responsive to our desires, now comes fully into operation. Our earthly life, completed by death, judges itself by producing an environment for the next stage of our existence which is determined by the quality of our character at the time of death. In general and for most of us that next stage will be purgatorial. For as our desires are uninhibitedly fulfilled their true value will be revealed to us, and in many cases we shall become profoundly dissatisfied with the world which we have made for ourselves. For frequently our dominating desires are extremely trivial from the point of view of richness of emotional and intellectual content so that their unlimited fulfilment must lead to the terrible *accidie* of boredom. Furthermore, depth psychology has revealed to us that we harbour many ugly and destructive desires which are at present repressed but which will have their way and work themselves out in a world which is formed by our wishes out of the material provided by memory. Again we have conflicting desires, so that there may be aspects of the next world which gratify our worse nature while being agonizingly repellent to our better nature; or which are welcomed by our better but spoiled by the power of our lower desires.

However, if the self-created world which fulfils an individual's wishes is to him hellish rather than heavenly it may thereby work for his salvation. For it may sooner or later evoke in him a yearning for something better, a longing for a more valuable and ultimately more satisfying existence. He may begin to 'hunger and thirst after righteousness'; and then his desire will lead him on into higher worlds and perhaps finally to a total purification from evil desire and a final entry into the conscious presence of infinite Goodness. This will be eternal life, the life of the kingdom of God, supervening upon a long and perhaps arduous approach both in this world and in other worlds to come.

These alternative ways of thinking are each capable of expressing different elements in Jesus' teaching concerning the after-life, and I shall presently suggest how they may be woven together in the conception of many lives in many worlds.

2 *On being mortal*

Although it is entirely proper and appropriate when we are trying to think about the nature of the universe and the place of human life within it to emphasize the Christian hope of eternal life, yet we still have to give our main attention to this present world and the problems of living within it. For as well as being immortal we are also mortal! And our immediate task is to live well the present life which is all that we are now allowed to see.

Those who are young – in their teens or twenties – generally have not yet realized that they *are* mortal! Of course they know that all humans are mortal and that they are human, and they draw the logical conclusion. But this is not the same as being conscious with the whole being, and as a fact to be reckoned with, that you personally are in due course going to die. It is possible when young even to go through a great war without really believing in your own mortality. (I had my own twenty-second birthday on a troop ship that was being attacked by submarines just outside the Straits of Gibraltar; but neither then nor at any other time during those war years did I *feel* mortal.) Indeed it is very commonly only when we are approaching the half-way point of life that we become consciously mortal. This is no doubt one of the factors that tends to set a gulf between the older and younger age groups – for what bigger difference could there be than that the one group consists of immortals and the other of mortals? And yet even this communication barrier need not be insuperable; for those who are now mortal can remember the time when they were immortal and should be able to converse with those who are still in that paradisal state.

We come next to an observation addressed to those who are old, those who in Britain are called old-age pensioners and who in the United States of America have the much nicer title of senior citizens. It is perhaps worth saying that the experience of dying is – so far as observation can tell – not usually anything to be dreaded. When it comes at the natural end of the life span as the organism is wearing out death is usually not unwelcome. For the dying person, his bodily frame having done its work, is usually at that stage so tired and so reduced in vitality that in the end he or she slips thankfully away from consciousness and from this life with the relief of an utterly exhausted person dropping gratefully to sleep. At that last stage, death, so far from being feared or resisted, is welcome. A physician and psychiatrist writes:

> The moment of death is not often a crisis of distress for the dying person. For most, the suffering is over a while before they die. Already some of the living functions have failed and full consciousness usually goes early. Before the last moments of life there comes a quieter phase of surrender, the body appears to abdicate peacefully, no longer attempting to survive. Life then slips away so that few are aware of the final advent of their own death.[3]

The experience of dying then, when it comes at the right time, is (so far as we can tell by observing it) usually neither painful or frightening. Of course if it comes prematurely through painful disease or shocking accident or violence, this is a very different matter. But these situations apart, when death is close at hand in the natural course of nature it has usually ceased to appear as an enemy and is accepted as a friend.

However, let us turn from that last phase to that great bulk of life which is lived between youth and old age. What is here the Christian attitude to our mortality and to the mortality of those whom we love?

It is here that God's gift of eternal life can affect and colour the sense of our mortality. Death is still indeed a solemn matter. As entry into the unknown, into 'that undiscovered country from whose bourne no traveller returns', it will always be met with a certain profound and solemn awe and apprehension – awe and apprehension in face of a great mystery. But it should not evoke the sickening fear with which we face what we know to be evil. For the one thing that as Christians we do know about what lies on the other side of death is that it is not evil but good. It is a fuller stage in the outworking of the Creator's loving purpose for his children.

Of course we know nothing concrete about the conditions of our existence after death. We have a few hints on the basis of which we can speculate, as we shall be doing in the following sections. Amid the hints what we have firmly and clearly is the indication given by Jesus, chiefly in parables, that beyond death there lies ultimately the fulfilment of God's good purpose for his children. This fulfilment is called in the New Testament the kingdom of God, and it is pictured in very earthly terms as a great banquet in which all and sundry rejoice together in dancing and gladness. The point does not of course lie in the details of the picture of the messianic banquet, for they are simply clues to something beyond our present range of experience. The point lies rather in the basic character of the kind of picture that Jesus chose to use. He did not, like some of our hymns and prayers, use symbols suggesting that eternal life is negative, static and essentially pointless and boring. He used symbols pointing to eternal life as limitlessly enhanced life, as a state of being more intensely alive in an existence which is both perfect fulfilment and yet also endless activity and newness. If death leads eventually to *that*, then although we shall still think of it both for ourselves and for others with trembling awe and apprehension, yet it will not evoke terror or despair; for beyond death we and they will not be less alive but more alive than we are now.

But let me ask this question, which is provoked by what I have just been saying: if God's gift to mankind is not only life but unlimited life, what is the purpose of death? Why should we die at all if it is only to live again beyond death? Why have we our animal mortality if we are really to enjoy eternal life?

Here is a suggestion. Perhaps death serves, but in a bigger way, a function like that of sleep. Sleep cuts life up for us into small manageable sections. Even if we did not need sleep for physical rest we should still need it to divide life into parts that we can cope with. We could not face an endless continuity of consciousness, an unceasing bombardment of sense impressions, continual activity without respite. Life would be intolerably intense if we did not after each eighteen or so hours relapse into unconsciousness and then begin again the next day. Without that periodic disengagement in sleep we should be so continuously up against the world and one another and all life's complexities and problems that we might well break down under the unremitting pressure. Sleep is indeed a beneficent provision of nature. As so often Shakespeare has perfectly expressed it:

> Sleep that knits up the ravel'd sleave of care,
> The death of each day's life, sore labour's bath,
> Balm of hurt minds, great nature's second course,
> Chief nourisher in life's feast –

chief nourisher because it gives us an ever renewed appetite for life's feast.

Perhaps the dividing-up function of sleep suggests a similar function for death in dividing up our immortal existence. Perhaps we could not at present face an endless vista of life but need the termination of death to circumscribe our life and make it manageable. Perhaps the function of death is to give us, at the present stage of our spiritual growth, a portion of life that we can cope with. In his play *Back to Methuselah* Bernard Shaw's Adam before the fall contemplates the prospect of an unending continuance of life and is appalled by it. 'It is the horror', he says, 'of having to be with myself for ever. I like you (he says to Eve); but I do not like myself. I want to be different; to be better; to begin again and again; to shed myself as a snake sheds its skin. I am tired of myself. And yet I must endure myself, not for a day or for many days, but for ever. That is a dreadful thought.'[4] I think Bernard Shaw was right. We should not want to live for ever and ever as we now are. It is better to have the limited period of our earthly life, in which we strive as best we can, and then for God to end it and move us on to another and different stage. The boundary of death gives us this present finite life to concentrate upon without being able to look beyond it. It sets a task before our eyes and under our hands. Our mortality presents us with an enclosed horizon, a limited vista of existence, often some sixty to eighty years, long enough for the largest human plans and achievements, and yet short enough for life to have a shape, a direction, an urgency. Because time is limited it is precious. Because we do not live in this world for ever we have to get on with whatever we are going to do.

If this is the purpose for which God has established our mortality how should we respond to that purpose? We are made mortal so that this earthly life shall have its full weight and value and urgency; we should then live it to the full as the life that God has given us to concentrate upon. We should accept the circumscribing horizon which death creates and live wholeheartedly within it, seeing each day with its new tasks and opportunities as something precious to be seized before it is gone. We should accept our mortality not as a limitation but as a means of concentration, and live fully in the present moment that God has given us, that extended moment whose duration is the duration of a human life. Although as Christians we know that this life will be caught up into eternity, we should live it as though it were complete in itself with nothing else beyond it. We are not to try to peer past it seeking to gain rewards or to avoid penalties beyond the frontier of death. This life is meant to stand validly on its own earthly feet.

We should, then, accept our mortality as something that God has ordained in his wise love and so live that like the best humanists we can say: 'I do not at present *mind* whether there is an after-life or not; I do not need one to make this life acceptable, for it is acceptable already in its own right.' And if we have been at all fortunate in the circumstances of our lives we can readily say this. Even if we believed that death is annihilation we should still be profoundly pleased with life. One must add, however, that there have always been those who bear much more than their share of the world's suffering, to whom this life is only a very qualified blessing and for whom it is in order to dwell upon the life to come. But for most of us God's gift of immortality is to remain during this life a hidden blessing, a future bonus, a background thought that does not obscure the immediacy and importance and vividness of the present moment.

For in giving us our present mortal life God has appointed *this* as the place and time of our recognition of his goodness towards us, which is salvation. In each present moment God, unseen, is seeking our response. The call to respond to God is immediate and urgent – not because the doors of salvation are going to be shut at the moment of death but because the discovery of God means also our own fulfilment and joy. We need no further reason and no later day to accept our highest good.

3 *Many lives in many worlds*

The way in which the boundary of death gives life its shape may well be significant in relation to the character of continued existence after death.

What form or forms might such continued life take? If it is to serve the person-making purpose which we are postulating, there must be continued personal identity, including self-awareness and memory; and there must be continued moral life, in the sense of continued decision-making within situations which demand real ethical choices. This seems to entail that the life to come be a life lived in interaction with other people within a common environment. And this in turn implies a temporal existence; for human interactions and the making of moral choices are events that occur in temporal sequence.

Should we then think of the life to come as a single prolonged existence stretching in time from the end of the present earthly life to the eventual attainment of human perfection? Such a span would have to be truly immense. For when we consider the contrast between the general moral and spiritual quality of human life now, and that of the great souls among us who are nearest to human perfection, we are bound to think of any intermediate life linking the two as immensely long. In earthly time we have to think in terms not of years but perhaps of centuries. The length of such an intermediate existence will presumably vary for different individuals; for some seem to grow as persons faster than others. But we can see that for the generality of mankind the 'distance' to be traversed between our present state and our eventual perfection must require the equivalent, not of one more earthly life, but of many many such lives, perhaps in the order of tens or hundreds. It is, then, in relation to a temporal span of this order that we ask whether we are to think of it as one single continuous existence or as divided up into a number of lives lived one after the other?

The latter possibility represents the basic hypothesis of the religions of Indian origin. Hinduism and Buddhism both teach that for the perfecting of the human self (which for them is its transcending of individual egoity) a single human life is not enough, and that the individual must live again and again, carrying forward his *karma* from life to life. Hinduism and Buddhism teach that the on-going individual karmic history enters into the formation of successive human lives, so that our deeper self is reborn or reincarnated again and again on earth. But the basic idea that our total existence is divided up into a series of limited phases is not tied to this Eastern belief in repeated reincarnations in this world. The alternative is some kind of doctrine of what might be called vertical reincarnation (i.e. reincarnation in an ascending series of environments beyond this earth) in distinction from doctrines of horizontal reincarnation (i.e. reincarnation along the plane of earthly history).

But what is the case for postulating a divided rather than a continuous existence after the present life, whether such a divided existence be in this or in other worlds? The basic case is that – as we saw in the last section – human moral and spiritual growth presuppose boundaries to existence such as our mortality provides. Consider again the way in which the termination of death gives shape and meaning to a human life. Moral and spiritual person-making seem to require a finite and bounded, or at any rate horizoned and therefore apparently bounded, context. Within the horizon of the three or four score years of a human life we exist responsibly, our actions matter, our choices are important, opportunities must be seized or lost, life is 'real', and for good or ill we develop as persons. As a dramatist's play has to concentrate attention upon a particular thread or knot of human experience, within a certain limited span of space and time, so the dramatic unity of a human life requires a certain temporal shape, with a beginning, middle and end. But if we lived continuously for ever, or for an enormously long period of thousands or millions of years, it is very hard to see how there could be any boundary-pressure such as makes possible the growth and development of the moral personality. It is precisely because we do not live for ever that our life has a certain urgency which gives it point and meaning. For the temporality of life as we know it is not an endless flow into a limitless future, but a movement towards an end. Our human existence is, in Heidegger's haunting phrase, being-towards-death. And so the present moment is precious: if we are ever to achieve anything, we have to get on with it:

> The Bird of Time has but a little way
> To fly! and Lo! the Bird is on the wing.[5]

It is this awareness of the irreversible passage of time that gives both poignancy and preciousness to love and loyalty, to purposes and achievements, and to the characteristic values of childhood, youth, maturity and old age. We have to engage with the tasks and problems of human life and history as they are taking place around us now; and it is in and through this activity, geared to the changing pattern of human affairs in time, that moral decisions are made, that character is created, and that a relationship with God may be established.

I do not claim that these considerations point decisively to a series of lives rather than a single prolonged existence in the period between death and the ultimate state of mankind. But such considerations seem to me to support a likelihood on the basis of which it is reasonable to proceed, if we propose to speculate at all about a life or lives to come.

But at this point let us turn from the very broad philosophical considerations which seem to point to the likelihood of many post-mortem lives, to the evidence of a very interesting and important work, the *Bardo Thödol* or Tibetan Book of the Dead.[6] This is a book, based on Mahayana Buddhist traditions, giving instruction to a dying person about what to expect during the comparatively short period between his present life, now ending, and his next incarnation, which may be in this or another world. The information is supposedly based upon yogic memories of this *bar-do*, or between two, state. The document described how the consciousness, after separation from the body, encounters a series of good and kindly, and then evil and destructive, deities who seek to draw it up or down into their own heavenly or purgatorial worlds. It is explained that these experiences are all projections of the individual's own imagination. The good and evil aspects of his personality are revealing themselves and their respective strengths in an experience of self-revelation and self-judgment. The particular form which this experience takes in the mind of a devout Tibetan Buddhist, as described in the *Bardo Thödol*, is determined by the complex tantric mythology. The distinctively Christian, Muslim, Jewish and Hindu forms of the *bardo* experience would be characteristically different. But in each case, if the indications in the *Bardo Thödol* should turn out to be true, one's consciousness immediately after death is in a subjective, dream-like state (such as was referred to above, pp. 107f.) in which one is offered a greater self-awareness, expressed – in the case of those whose minds have been sufficiently powerfully conditioned by a religious tradition – under symbols of divine judgment.

If this is indeed the kind of post-mortem experience undergone by minds deeply imbued with positive religious expectations, what might be the experience of the secular mind of our post-religious Western societies? The only evidence we have, if it is indeed evidence at all, comes from supposed communications from the dead through trance mediumship and automatic writing. I am very far from saying that all of these, or even that some of these, are to be accepted as what they profess to be. I think however that it is not inconceivable that, if human consciousness continues to exist after bodily death, there may be occasional telepathic interactions between embodied and disembodied minds, and that such interactions may be a factor within some of these mediumistic communications. It would at any rate, I think, be an unwarrantably dogmatic stance to rule this out altogether. And if there are in these supposed communications any indications of the state of mind of some who have recently died, these indications seem in general to agree with those of the *Bardo Thödol*, given the important difference that strong religious expectations are no longer widespread in our post-Christian Western culture. Very often the dead (if such they are) who communicate through mediums seem to find their next world very like this earth – so much so that they can sometimes at first hardly believe that they have died. And if the world that they experience is a dream-like construction created, in default of any powerful religious imagery, out of their memories of this world, this is perhaps just what we might expect.

At any rate, if we take note of these possible indications from the *Bardo Thödol* and from Western spiritualist communications, and relate them to the religious belief that the universe exists to serve a soul-making or person-making purpose, we can form the following very general hypothesis. At death, mental life continues after the cessation of physical life. And then, during a period which is presumably longer or shorter in different cases, it exists in the *bardo* state, which is a dream-like condition in which there is no new sensory input and in which, released from the pressures of an objective environment, the individual undergoes a kind of psychoanalytic experience of self-awareness and self-assessment. But this is only a temporary phase (lasting according to the *Bardo Thödol* for a symbolic period of 49 days). At the end of it, the individual is re-embodied, or reincarnated, in another spatial environment, which we can thus call a world. In thinking of further lives in other worlds rather than of further lives on this earth, as so many in the East believe, I am presupposing what seem to me to be weighty criticisms of the hypothesis of earthly reincarnation.[7] Admittedly, such arguments present us with a likelihood rather than a proof. But whilst there may be occasional exceptional instances of individuals being born again in this world, suggested by some of the reports of ostensible memories of a previous life, the general likelihood seems to me to be that any further lives beyond the *bardo* state occur in other worlds. And if we ask – as we must – where these other worlds are, the likelihood seems to me to be that each is in its own space. Thus we are led to postulate spaces in the plural. If we then ask, from within space number one, where the objects in space number two are, the answer has to be that they are nowhere; for an object in space number two is not at any distance or in any direction from an object in space number one. And of course, from the point of view of an inhabitant of a world in space number two, objects in space number one are nowhere. There is however the difference, according to our hypothesis, that an inhabitant of space number two may have memories of having existed in another world, which was in space number one. We are thus involved in speaking of plural spaces and singular time; and of a movement from life to life in different worlds, with a disembodied *bardo* phase at the transition from one world to the next.

What the character may be of later embodiments in world after world we can have no notion. It need not be assumed either that our bodily size, shape and appearance will be like or that it will be unlike our present embodiment. Again, whether one enters the next world, and the next after that, and so on, as an immature creature, like a baby being born into this world, or as a mature inhabitant of that world, can be left open in our hypothesis. So, again, can the question of the degree of memory that is carried forward in each transition; though the analogy of our present memory would suggest that there would be at least a minimal thread of memory from life to life.

Leaving these, and many other, questions unanswered, we can consider the broad hypothesis of many lives in many worlds as a system which makes possible the gradual growth of the human self towards its perfection. No doubt during this long journey from human animal to child of God there is regress as well as progress; and probably there is not just one route from world to world, followed by everyone, but many different routes. A great variety of pictures is possible within our general hypothesis. What must however be said within all these variations is that each world will be a real environment, functioning in accordance with its own laws, and having its own history and its own pressing concerns and exigencies, within which real decisions have to be made, with real consequences, through which we can grow or fail to grow as persons. To some extent the contemporary Western imagination has recently been stretched by science fiction to encompass the idea of many worlds with perhaps utterly different concrete conditions of existence. And each life is to be thought of as a complete episode in itself, with its own beginning and end, within which we are intended to live, wholeheartedly involved in its concerns. Only occasionally is it wise to stand back for a moment from life's urgent tasks, as we are now doing, to contemplate the long pilgrimage within which we may now be only at an early stage.

4 *The ultimate unity of mankind before God*

When we do pause to contemplate this long journey through time, we see that however long it may be it leads eventually to something else beyond it.

According to our hypothesis the individual has, through a series of lives, progressed towards his human perfection, which is the fulfilment of his potentialities as a child of God. Christianity has depicted this ultimate eschatological state, beyond our long pilgrimage in time, under two rather different sets of images. One is a set of social images: the kingdom of heaven, the city of God, the messianic banquet, the communion of saints, the new Jerusalem. Here man's ultimate state is pictured as an ideal community living consciously in the divine presence. And within this community men retain their separate individualities, with its basis in their separate bodies existing outside one another in a spatial environment. The other set of images suggests individual mystical absorption into the life of God: above all, the image of the vision of God, in which the human self, apparently no longer embodied, is aware of God in a way which completely fills his consciousness to the exclusion of all else. An image which is used by some of the mystics, speaking of this ultimate unitive state, is that of a piece of iron placed inside a burning furnace: the iron is so penetrated by the fiery heat that it becomes red hot and glows with fire, being thus still a separate entity and yet at the same time now a part of the fire. The Indian religions also have their images of man's ultimate state. In the monistic thought of advaita Vedanta, human individuality is an illusion, and when this illusion is transcended the universal Self continues its eternal existence, but now free from this illusion of finitude and multiplicity. On some interpretations the Buddhist concept of *nirvana* is very similar to this; though it is a mysterious and varied concept, with interpretations varying from sheer non-existence to union with an eternal spiritual reality. The other type of imagery in the Indian religions is that of the theistic-devotional traditions, with the *Bhagavad Gita* as their central scripture. Here the individual remains distinct from God, though brought into an intimate personal communion with him, with created life being lived within the life of God.

It might seem that in the face of these options we have to choose one and reject the others. But on the other hand if we see these various eschatological images, not as definitive doctrines but as pointers to an unknown reality which lies beyond our vision, we can I think see that they may well be pointing convergingly.

Let us start at the Western end. The ultimate state consists in man's individual perfecting in relation to God. But in what direction does this perfection lie? The ancient and medieval conception of personality was as a psychic atom, an individual rational entity or substance. Today we are more conscious of the interpersonal nature of personality. Being a person is not an inherent quality possessed by the isolated individual. There can be no such thing as a completely and permanently solitary person, because personality exists in interaction with other persons. To be a person is to be part of a system of relationships. In short, personality is essentially interpersonal.

We can in fact distinguish between two aspects of the self, the self as ego and the self as person, which exist in a tension which is the basis of our moral nature. The self as ego is an autonomous and self-protective unit, programmed for individual survival. Self-concern is the natural standpoint of the self as ego; and as egos we naturally want to live for ever. What traditional theology has called our fallenness, or our original sinfulness, is our egoity. On the other hand, the self as personal exists in relationship to others. It is essentially outward-looking and other-regarding. The demands and delights of personal relationship lead it out of itself to live in sensitive, vulnerable interaction with others. It lives in community; and it gives itself to others within the common life.

Could it be that the gradual perfecting of the human self, which is in traditional language its salvation, consists in its becoming more and more a person and less and less an ego? Could salvation be a progressive transcending of the boundaries of egoity to enter ever more deeply into the common life of humanity? Could it be that our true life, as we eventually find it, will not be as separate egos, each excluding the others, but as members one of another in the unitary life of mankind in relation to God? The ancient Hindu conception of the Atman points towards such fulfilment. For it is taught that in the deepest depth of our being we are all one, and that our present separate existences are an illusion created by egoity. So long as the self lives the life of the ego, it knows itself as a distinct and bounded unit. But when it voluntarily overcomes all selfishness and self-seeking it then knows itself as the universal Atman which it truly is, the illusion of separate egoity having faded away. And many of the Christian mystics have also pointed in this same direction when they have spoken of the self-naughting, the casting off of all egoism, in the soul's movement towards God. For when we cast off our separating egoisms we shall become one with all other souls in the common life of perfected humanity.

At this point, different eschatological models offer themselves. There is the model of the complete absorption of the individual in the larger reality, like a raindrop falling into the ocean, with no element of plurality left. But here we may, I would suggest, point as Christians to an alternative model offered by the doctrine of the Trinity. In certain forms of the trinitarian doctrine, the three Persons of the Holy Trinity are three persons in the sense of three centres of conscious personal life. They are not however three egos, each autonomous and only externally related to one another. Rather they form a community of persons so total and intimate as to be three in one and one in three. Each lives in the others in a complex personal life of a higher order than our own. May not this notion of unity in plurality and plurality in unity perhaps apply to the ultimate state of mankind, in which all egoity has been transcended and the unitary life of humanity as a whole has been realized? This life will then constitute a human community so intimate as to be many-in-one and one-in-many.

The overall picture would then be one of man's emergence out of the primal psychic unity of primitive tribes, in which there is virtually no individuality but rather a collective tribal mind, into the dangerous but creative phase of individual freedom and responsibility, and then finally the free self-directed return to unity, but at a higher level. And the phase in which we now are, the phase of the history of interacting egos, is one in which we may gradually come, as we pass through this and other worlds, voluntarily to overcome and transcend our own egoity in the realization of true human community.

At any rate this seems to me to be a possible picture of the human future, and one which appears to make religious and moral sense, and which is moreover consonant with the converging hints offered by the major religious traditions of West and East.[8]

NOTES

1. Out of the vast literature on this subject I would recommend especially Benjamin Wolman, ed., *Handbook of Parapsychology* (Van Nostrand, 1977), and C. D. Broad, *Lectures on Psychical Research* (London: Routledge & Kegan Paul, and New York: Humanities Press, 1962). A useful first introduction addressed to Christians is E. Garth Moore, *Believe it or not: Christianity and Psychical Research* (London: Mowbray, 1977).

2. H. H. Price, 'Personal Survival and the Idea of "Another World",' *Proceedings of the Society for Psychical Research*, January 1953; reprinted in J. R. Smythies, ed., *Brain and Mind*, London: Routledge & Kegan Paul, and New York: Humanities Press, 1965.

3. John Hinton, *Dying*, London and New York: Penguin, 1967, p. 77.

4. G. B. Shaw, *Back to Methuselah*, Harmondsworth and Baltimore: Penguin, 1971, p. 71.

5. *Rubáiyát of Omar Khayyám*, quatrain VII.

6. W. Y. Evans-Wentz, ed., *The Tibetan Book of the Dead*, London and New York: Oxford University Press, 1960; or Francesca Fremantle and Chogyam Trungpa, trans. *The Tibetan Book of the Dead*, Berkeley Cal., and London: Shambhala Publications, 1975.

7. See e.g. my *Death and Eternal Life*, London: Collins, 1976, and New York: Harper & Row, 1977, chs. 16–19.

8. The ideas in this chapter are developed more fully in my *Death and Eternal Life*.

For Further Reading

Hans Küng, *On Being a Christian*, New York: Doubleday, 1976, and London: Collins, 1977. A comprehensive modern view of Christianity by a liberal Roman Catholic theologian.

Maurice Wiles, *The Remaking of Christian Doctrine*, London: SCM Press, 1974, and Philadelphia: Westminster Press, 1978. An important contemporary restatement.

Dennis Nineham, *The Use and Abuse of the Bible*, London: Macmillan, and New York: Barnes & Noble, 1976; London: SPCK paperback, 1977. An important new discussion of the place of the Bible within Christianity.

John Knox, *The Humanity and Divinity of Christ*, Cambridge and New York: Cambridge University Press, 1967. An illuminating book by a distinguished New Testament scholar.

Wilfred Cantwell Smith, *The Meaning and End of Religion*, revised ed., San Francisco: Harper & Row, and London: SPCK, 1978. A modern classic of religious studies.

Wilfred Cantwell Smith, *Towards a World Theology*, London: Macmillan, and Philadelphia: Westminster Press, 1981. A fascinating pointer to the future.

Index

Orthodoxy, 70ff.

Pascal, Blaise, 44, 48
Pluralism, 71, 82–91
Popper, Karl, 113
Predestination, 102

Rahner, Karl, 80
Reality, 83–90
Reincarnation, 128ff.
Religion, 23f.
Robinson, John, 71
Russell, Bertrand, 13, 39, 94

Saints, 82, 87f.
Salvation, 77–80, 86, 101
Schillebeeckx, Edward, 71
Schlick, Moritz, 112f.
Science and religion, 102–109
Science fiction, 35ff.
Shakespeare, William, 125
Shaw, Bernard, 125

Sleep, 124f.
State, the, 21f.
Stendhal, 93
Suffering, 12, 93f., 98f.

Theology, conservative, 9f., 74
    evangelical, 9
    of religions, 77–82
    radical, 10
Tibetan Book of the Dead,
    129f.

Universality, 79, 80, 92
Unorthodoxy, 70ff.

Verification, 109f.
    eschatological, 111ff.

Warren, Max, 104f.
Wittgenstein, Ludwig, 45
World religions, 76–91
    Christian attitude to, 76ff.